Faith,
Skepticism,
and Evidence

Faith, Skepticism, and Evidence

An Essay in Religious Epistemology

Stephen T. Davis

Lewisburg
Bucknell University Press
London: Associated University Presses

© 1978 by Associated University Presses, Inc.

Associated University Presses, Inc.
Cranbury, New Jersey 08512

Associated University Presses
Magdalen House
136-148 Tooley Street
London SE1 2TT, England

Library of Congress Cataloging in Publication Data

Davis, Stephen T   1940–
    Faith, skepticism, and evidence.

    Bibliography: p.
    Includes index.
    1. Knowledge, Theory of (Religion)   I. Title.
BL51.D364   230   76-49784
ISBN 0-8387-2039-0

Contents

Preface

This essay is an attempt to answer two questions, What is the nature of religious faith?, and Is religious faith ever justified? One traditional way of approaching both questions is to speak of the relationship between faith and reason. I wish to take a different route and deal instead with the relationship between faith and *evidence*. This is a slightly different approach from the one that most epistemologists of religion have taken, but I believe that it will prove fruitful in determining exactly what faith is and whether or not faith is ever justified or rationally warranted.

Traditionally, a distinction has been made in theology between a cognitive and a noncognitive aspect of faith. The noncognitive aspect is *fiducia*: an attitude of trust in and commitment to God. The other side of faith is *fides*: a cognitive or propositional state, comparable to belief or knowledge, in which certain propositions are accepted or believed. Since this essay is primarily an epistemological rather than a theological study, my main concern will be with *fides;* only occasionally will I speak about *fiducia*.

This study is located, so to speak, on the boundary between two traditional areas of philosophy, namely, epistemology and philosophy of religion. Epistemology is the science or study of knowledge. It asks such questions as, What is knowledge? What can be known and how can it be known? What is truth? What is perception, and is perception a reliable source of knowledge? How does knowledge differ from such other cognitive states as belief, opinion, doubt, hope, or faith? The subtitle "An Essay in Religious Epistemology" expresses my aim to describe and evaluate cognitive claims in the area of religion.

Philosophy of religion is concerned with philosophical scrutiny of religion. It is not (as some medieval philosophers viewed it) a philosophical defense of religion, nor is it (as some modern philosophers view it) a philosophical attack on religion. Philosophy of religion attempts to reach rational conclusions about religion, whether they be in favor of or against religion. Philosophy itself is ideologically neutral: it accepts whatever conclusions are rationally defensible, whatever arguments are strongest. Philosophy of religion attempts (1) to analyze such concepts typically used in religious discourse as *God, evil, death, eternal life, miracle, soul, creation, omnipotence,* and the like, and (2) to evaluate various arguments that have been advanced for and against religious claims.

This work is written primarily from a Christian perspective; indeed, I am a Christian believer. I am sure that my claims about the nature and justification of religious faith can equally well apply to other religions, but it is probably inevitable that works in philosophy of religion be written primarily from the perspective of the religion the author knows best. However, the study should not be viewed as a work of Christian apologetics, at least not in the traditional sense of this term. It is not an attempt to argue that the propositions Christians accept "on faith" are evident, and no arguments along these lines will be advanced. It is a work of apologetics only in the restricted sense that I will attempt to show what religious faith is and that in certain circumstances it is intellectually justified.

In Part I I set the stage for my analysis and defense of religious faith. I introduce and discuss the notions of knowledge, evidence, rationality, philosophical skepticism, religious skepticism, faith, and religious faith. Inspired in part by arguments of ancient skeptics such as Sextus Empiricus, I introduce a type of philosophical skepticism that I call "adequate skepticism" and argue that adequate skepticism can be refuted only by an appeal to pragmatic considerations. I argue that all knowledge is ultimately based on faith.

Part II is a detailed and careful evaluation of William James's argument in favor of religious faith in his famous essay "The Will To Believe" and other of his early essays. Many philosophers believe that James's argument is fallacious, but I argue that it is sound, if interpreted correctly. In chapters 5 and 6 I state and clarify James's general thesis; in chapters 7 and 8 I defend it against criticism; and in chapter 9 I apply it to religious faith.

In Part III I do two main things. First, in chapter 10, I attempt to reply to the charge that faith propositions are cognitively meaningless; and second, in chapter 11, I make use of James's argument and the conclusions of Part I to show that religious faith is in some circumstances epistemologically justified.

Acknowledgments

I have been thinking the thoughts expressed in this study —or their ancestors—for a long time. I first began asking epistemological questions about the rationality of religious faith as an undergraduate in college under Professor Howard A. Redmond of Whitworth College. Already I was beginning to wonder: How is faith related to evidence? Later I was exposed to the rationalism of the late Professor Edward J. Carnell of Fuller Theological Seminary, a kind and helpful man as well as an invigorating teacher, whose views on faith and evidence I now largely reject, but whose memory I cherish. Still later, at Princeton Theological Seminary, I studied under Professor John H. Hick, whose influences on this essay will be obvious to the reader. I would also like to thank Professor John H. Hutchison of Claremont Graduate School and my colleagues Professors John K. Roth and Steven A. Smith of Claremont Men's College. Their encouragement and criticisms and probing questions have signally improved this effort, though of course I alone am responsible for any errors and deficiencies.

Much of the writing of this essay was completed during the summer of 1974 under the sponsorship of a Claremont Men's College Summer Fellowship. I would like to thank those who supervised the awarding of these fellowships for the support it provided. I would also like to thank Mrs. Pat Gayler and Mrs. Marti Simmons, the philosophy secretaries at Claremont Men's College, for their faithful and accurate typing of the manuscript.

I would like to thank the following for permission to reprint copyrighted material:

Association Press, for material from *Exploring the Logic of Faith*, by K. Bendall and F. Ferre, copyright 1962.

Basil Blackwell & Mott Ltd, for material from " 'The Will To Believe' Revisited," by Robert W. Beard, *Ratio* 8 (December 1966).

Cornell University Press, for material reprinted from John Hick: *Faith and Knowledge*. First edition copyright 1957, second edition copyright © 1966 by Cornell University. Used by permission of Cornell University Press.

Dover Publications, Inc. for material from *Charles S. Peirce: Selected Writings*, ed. Philip Wiener, copyright 1966.

New Jersey: Humanities Press, Inc., for material from *Evidence and Meaning*, by Robert V. Fogelin, copyright 1967.

International Journal for Philosophy of Religion 6, no. 1 (Spring 1975), for permission to use much of "Theology, Verification, and Falsification," by Stephen T. Davis.

Routledge & Kegan Paul Ltd., for material from *Evidence and Meaning*, by Robert V. Fogelin, copyright 1967.

Transactions of the Charles Peirce Society 8, no. 4 (Fall 1972), for permission to use much of "Wishful Thinking and 'The Will To Believe,' " by Stephen T. Davis.

Faith,
Skepticism,
and Evidence

Part I

Skepticism and Evidence

I

Evidence and Rationality

Let us define the term *evidence-situation* as any circumstance in which a person wonders whether or not a given proposition is true, or wants to argue either for or against a proposition. Evidence-situations are very common. Typically, they occur when the truth of a given proposition is challenged.

The man in the blue suit is Jones.
Are you sure? I think it's Smith.

Today is March 30th.
No, it's the 29th.

A loving God exists.
Possibly, but I don't see much evidence.

Clearly, the type and degree of evidence the defender or critic of the proposition will need to elicit will vary greatly from situation to situation. Consider, for example, the various kinds and degrees of evidence that would be required to confirm or disconfirm the following propositions.

(1)   The man in the blue suit is Jones.
(2)   Today is March 30th.
(3)   A loving God exists.
(4) $2 + 2 = 4$.

    (5)   Every event has a cause.
    (6)   Water at sea level boils at 212 degrees Fahrenheit.
    (7)   The Dodo is extinct.
    (8)   Ireland is a beautiful country.
    (9)   This exam deserves an "A".
   (10)   The patient is suffering from cancer.
   (11)   The defendant is guilty of murder.
   (12)   This piece of pottery is from second-century Palestine.

There are a wide variety of evidence-situations that occur in human experience, and a wide variety of ways of confirming or disconfirming propositions. What constitutes "adequate evidence" for a proposition or "good reasons" for belief in a proposition varies greatly from case to case. (The expressions *adequate evidence for p* and *good reasons for belief in p* will be used virtually synonymously in this essay.)

It seems to me that our behavior in evidence-situations is loosely based on an assumption that normally remains unstated, despite its tacit acceptance by anyone who wants to be considered a "rational" person. Let us call this assumption "Russell's Principle," for Bertrand Russell offers a clear formulation of what I take this assumption to be:[1]

> Give to any hypothesis that is worth your while to consider just that degree of credence which the evidence warrants.

This Principle, or something very like it, appears to be one of our accepted criteria of "rationality." Anyone who wants to be considered a rational person must allow the Principle to guide him in evidence-situations. That is, he must base his beliefs on evidence. Anyone who violates the Principle by, for example, accepting a proposition that is not supported by evidence or rejecting a proposition that is supported by evidence, is considered irrational.

We can distinguish five main categories or cases of evidence-situations. That is, we can argue that any proposition p whose truth is wondered about or challenged will fit into one of the following five categories (or into one of the innumerable subcategories in between):

(1)   There is adequate evidence that p.

(2)   There is some evidence that p, but not adequate evidence
      that p. (Or the evidence that p outweighs the evidence
      that not-p, but not decisively.)

(3)   (a) There is no relevant evidence available, or (b) the
      evidence that p is neither stronger nor weaker than the
      evidence that not-p.

(4)   There is some evidence that not-p, but not adequate evi-
      dence that not-p. (Or the evidence that not-p outweighs
      the evidence that p, but not decisively.)

(5)   There is adequate evidence that not-p.

Roughly, it would appear that Russell's Principle dictates
the following cognitive attitudes toward p in the following
cases: in case (1) a firm commitment to the truth of p; in
case (5) a firm commitment to the truth of not-p; in case
(2) a tentative commitment to the truth of p; in case (4)
a tentative commitment to the truth of not-p; and in case
(3) a refusal to commit oneself at all.

What does the term *adequate evidence* mean? This is a
difficult question, and I do not propose to try to answer it
in detail. Let us simply say that evidence is adequate when
it is as good or convincing as it can or need be, when further
investigation into the truth of the proposition in question is
pointless. Thus the notion of adequate evidence is related
to the notion of justification or legitimacy. We have adequate evidence for p precisely when we are justified in
affirming p, when we have the right to be sure that p is
true. What determines whether or not evidence for a given
proposition is adequate? Notoriously, people will disagree
on this point. Let us say that what constitutes adequate
evidence is ultimately determined by the consensus of rational persons.

What constitutes adequate evidence will obviously vary
greatly from proposition to proposition and from context

to context. For example, it would normally take a great
deal more work to supply adequate evidence for a true proposition like "The patient is suffering from cancer" than for
a true proposition like "Today is March 30th." Or, take the
proposition "Jones was in Claremont at 11:30 last night."
It would obviously take a great deal more work for a de-
tective to find adequate evidence for this proposition (i.e.,
with his aim of compiling evidence to be used in court)
than it would for me (with my aim of simply satisfying my
curiosity where my friend Jones spent the night).

Where there is adequate evidence for p, a situation is
created where everyone (who is aware of the evidence)
should affirm p. This does not mean everyone *will*: people
behave irrationally on occasion. But the "should" is a moral
"should" in the realm of the ethics of belief: People should
(in order to behave rationally) accept propositions for which
there is adequate evidence.

There is also a broad spectrum of cases (cases 2 and 4
above) where there is relevant evidence available either for
or against a given proposition but where the available evidence fails to attain the standard of adequacy. In these cases
such locutions as these might be used:

There is some evidence that p.
It is probable that p.
I'm not sure, but I think that p.
I tend to believe that p.
p could be said.

Furthermore, there are a great variety of ways in which
it can be claimed that the evidence supporting a given person's belief fails to attain adequacy. One can claim that the
belief is "biased," meaning presumably that the belief is
influenced by other factors than the available evidence; or
one can claim that the belief is "dogmatic," meaning presumably that the belief is held much more firmly than the
evidence warrants; or one can claim that the belief is "one-
sided," meaning presumably that some of the evidence, es-

pecially evidence against the belief, is conveniently being ignored; or one can say that the belief is "old-fashioned" or "unscientific," meaning in one way or another that the present balance of evidence is not being adhered to; or one can claim that the belief is "naive" or "unsophisticated," meaning that it is a childish or immature belief held despite strong evidence to the contrary. In these and many other ways,[2] it can be claimed that the evidence supporting a belief is inadequate.

From time to time we encounter a proposition for which there appears to be no relevant evidence, either for or against it. More frequently, we encounter propositions for which the evidences pro and con seem evenly balanced. These kinds of cases will be discussed in detail later. Suffice it to say here that in such cases the convention is ordinarily that we suspend judgment on the truth of the proposition, that is, we believe neither it nor its negation. There is another possibility, too, however: We might accept (or reject) the proposition on some ground other than evidence. This second possibility, that of accepting or rejecting propositions for some reason other than the available evidence, will also be considered later.

As an ideal schema, the reasoning procedure that Russell's Principle dictates we follow in evidence-situations is roughly as follows: When a proposition is suggested and we must determine how much credence to place in it, (1) we first determine what kind of proposition it is and the context in which it is stated. (2) We then take into consideration the criteria of adequacy of evidence conventionally accepted for that sort of proposition in that context, that is, we consider what type, amount, and weight of evidence are required. (3) We then consider the actual evidence at hand for or against the proposition and measure it against the arrived-at standards of adequacy. (4) Finally, on the basis of the first three steps, we assign a degree of belief or unbelief to the proposition, that is, we place it in one of the five categories mentioned above (or in one of their subcategories).

This, I claim, is how Russell's Principle guides us. I do

not claim that we always or even often go through the steps consciously, and the schema is obviously oversimplified; in practice the reasoning is much more complex. I do claim, however, that some such procedure must be at work if ordinary language is to succeed in evidence-situations, that is, if people are to communicate with each other. For if there were no agreed-upon procedure we would not be able to understand what was being said when a given belief was called, say, *rational* or *warranted* or *biased* or *unscientific*. There must be a common frame of reference in evidence-situations, and that reference is Russell's Principle and the procedures it entails. I shall argue later that Russell's Principle is not always normative in evidence-situations. For now I simply wish to develop the criterion of rationality that the Principle clearly does constitute for us.

As can be seen, the notion of evidence plays an important role in determining criteria of rationality. Thus it might be helpful at this point to define the term *evidence*. Here there are difficulties, however. *Evidence* appears to be one of those terms which are used frequently in ordinary discourse and which are readily understood, but which are seldom carefully defined.

There are three distinct ways in which we might define *evidence*: what I will call the "behavioral definition," the "probability definition," and the "epistemic definition."

Behavioral Definition: Any proposition p is evidence for a hypothesis h when p tends to produce belief in h.

Probability Definition: Any proposition p is evidence for a hypothesis h when p makes h more probable.

Epistemic Definition: Any proposition p is evidence for a hypothesis h when p tends to justify belief in h.

I believe that support can be found for all three definitions, both in ordinary language and in philosophical argument, and it is not easy to decide which to accept. I will use the epistemic definition—it seems more illuminating to me than the others—and this will have an effect on the terminology I will use in developing the argument of this study. It will not significantly alter the content of the argument itself, however, which could have been stated in alternative ways had one of the other definitions instead been adopted.

The epistemic definition is not without its ambiguities. For example, the notion of *tending to justify belief in h* is not transparent and is perhaps dependent on some notion of probability: How better *justify* a belief than to show that it is a *probable* belief? But by the phrase *tend to justify belief in h* I mean that evidence for h will make belief in h epistemologically justified to the degree of the strength of the evidence. Adequate evidence for h will completely justify belief in h; inadequate evidence for h will give a degree of justification to belief in h that corresponds to the strength of the evidence.

Let us then stipulate that "Any proposition p is evidence for a hypothesis h when p tends to justify belief in h." I do not wish to claim that this is the only possible definition of the term, for alternative formulations seem quite possible. My hope is just that this definition is broad enough to cover the various uses of the term and will suffice for my purposes in this essay.

Let me now restate the five types of evidence-situations I described above in terms of the epistemic definition of *evidence*. There is adequate evidence for p when belief in p is as epistemologically justified as it can or need be, when belief in p has been rendered so acceptable that further investigation into the truth of p is pointless; there is inadequate evidence for p when belief in p has a degree of epistemological justification not so high as it can or need be, or not so as to render further investigation into p's truth pointless; and there is no evidence for p or the evidence for and against p is balanced when we are unable to make a judgment about the epistemological justification of belief in p or when the best judgment we can make about belief in p is that belief in p is no more and no less epistemologically justified than belief in not-p.

Near the end of the *Critique of Pure Reason,* in a section entitled "Opining, Knowing and Believing,"[3] Kant makes a distinction between grounds or reasons for belief that are (1) subjectively convincing and (2) objectively adequate. Opinion, Kant says, is a cognitive attitude that is both subjectively and objectively uncertain: the holder of the opinion knows that the grounds of his opinion are inadequate to render it knowledge, and in fact the grounds are inadequate. Knowledge, on the other hand, is a cognitive attitude that is both subjectively and objectively certain: the knower knows that the grounds of his knowledge are adequate to render it knowledge, and in fact the grounds are adequate. But belief or faith (the German word *Glauben* can be translated either way) is based on grounds that are subjectively convincing (they entirely convince the believer of the truth of his belief), but in fact they are objectively inadequate to render it knowledge.

People hold beliefs for a great variety of reasons, some of them good and some of them not so good. For example, take the proposition, "Edward Kennedy will run for President." Let us say that anyone who accepts this proposition holds the belief r (that Edward Kennedy will run for President). We can conceive of all sorts of reasons why a person might hold r.

Believer A: Holds r because Edward Kennedy sincerely told him that he was going to run for President.

Believer B: Holds r because his mailman, who does not know Edward Kennedy and who is not a recognized political expert, once said, "I'm sure Edward Kennedy is going to run for President."

Believer C: Holds r because he was indoctrinated by his anti-Kennedy parents to believe that "No Kennedy can ever pass up a chance to run for President."

Believer D: Holds r because it makes him feel good to hold r, that is, he loves Edward Kennedy and longs for him to run for President so he can work in his campaign, vote for him, etc.

It is clear that there are important epistemological differences between these beliefs and that we would rate them very differently on a rationality/irrationality scale.

Despite the convention that we should all follow Russell's Principle, it is obviously false to claim that we always do. I said earlier that we are justified in affirming a proposition when by the conventionally accepted criteria of adequacy we possess adequate evidence for that proposition. But I added that while everyone *should* accept propositions for which there is adequate evidence and reject propositions for whose negation there is adequate evidence, nevertheless not everyone does. People quite often base their attitudes toward propositions on some other ground than evidence. This is simply to make the point that other influences are sometimes at work than the available evidence in determining a person's attitude in evidence-situations: his wishes, feelings, prejudices, biases, and hopes are also often involved. Thus, paradoxically, I claim that while we all tacitly accept Russell's Principle as a basis for the acceptance or rejection of propositions, we also commonly break it (though we like to deny it when we are accused of breaking it).

In the light of the fact that people do commonly behave in this way, we can amend Russell's Principle slightly in order to create a principle that is not *normative,* as Russell's Principle is, but *descriptive* of the actual behavior of people in evidence-situations:

Give to any hypothesis that is worth your while to consider just that degree of credence which the evidence *as you see it* warrants.

This, and not the original version of Russell's Principle, is what I think people always follow. (As a normative canon of rationality, the original version still stands, however.) For it is a commonplace that when people make up their minds about the truth or falsity of a given proposition on other grounds than the balance of available evidence, they still quite typically can give reasons for their views. Thus we might even offer the following corollary:

No one ever believes anything contrary to what he sees as adequate evidence.

What I mean is simply that people typically do things for reasons, whether the reasons are good or bad, and that people act on *what they consider to be* good reasons, whether in fact the reasons are good or not. People believe only what they are convinced of, whether they are convinced by adequate evidential reasons, inadequate evidential reasons, or nonevidential reasons. (I am speaking here only of beliefs and am ignoring Kant's category of opinion.)

At this point, partly inspired by Kant, I wish to introduce a distinction between what I shall call *public reasons for belief* or *public evidence* and *private reasons for belief* or *private evidence*. Reasons for belief that are public are reasons that are *objective* (to use an admittedly ambiguous word). That is, they are open to the awareness and inspection of anyone who is interested enough to consider them, and they are transpersonal in their appeal. If adequate public reasons are presented in favor of a given proposition, the reasons should convince anyone of the truth of the proposition. For example, suppose someone invented a valid argument, based on known premises, that made highly probable the proposition *God exists*. This argument would constitute an adequate public reason for belief in the existence of God, for the argument would be open to the scrutiny of anyone who took time to analyze it, and the argument should convince anyone that he should accept the proposition *God exists*. Of course, someone could refuse to accept the conclusion, just as through sheer stupidity or stubbornness a person could deny that $2 + 2 = 4$. But unless he could show us a defect in the argument, we would have to agree that he is behaving irrationally, that he should accept the conclusion.

Adequate public evidence for p is evidence that should convince anyone that p: the consensus of rational people would consider it decisive. For example, I will take it that Believer A's belief in r is based on public reasons and, indeed, on adequate public reasons: what more adequate evidence could there be for r than the sincere word of Edward Kennedy himself? But the beliefs of Believers B, C, and D are based on private reasons, reasons that they alone find convincing. We will have to grant that B's belief is based on a genuine piece of public evidence for r (the word of the mailman), and so he can be said to have an "evidential reason for belief." But the increase in probability that the mailman's testimony gives to r is so slight as to be not only inadequate but virtually negligible. B then believes in r for private reasons, for he finds evidence convincing that the majority of rational persons would not find convincing. He is in violation of Russell's Principle. The beliefs of C and D appear to be based on nonevidential reasons: indoctrination and desire. They cannot count as public evidence at all for r (given our epistemic definition of evidence): if C and D do genuinely believe r because of the stated reasons, they believe for private reasons. They too are in violation of Russell's Principle: they are treating as convincing what the consensus of rational persons would not find convincing.

A person believes for a public reason, then, when whatever his belief is based upon would be counted as evidence by the consensus of rational persons; a person believes for a private reason when he believes either on the basis of inadequate public evidence or on the basis of some nonevidential reason (indoctrination, desire, prejudice, hypnosis, etc.) .

Private reasons for belief, then, are *subjective*. They are (at times, e.g., in ineffable experiences) open only to the awareness and scrutiny of the given individual to whom they are private, and are not necessarily convincing to anyone else (and should not convince anyone else). To return to the example of theistic belief, if a man believes in the existence of God not because of a theistic proof but because, say, his parents once told him that God exists, the parents' word is private evidence. The word was spoken only to the son, and was convincing only to the son. The second point is more important than the first as a criterion of privacy. Someone else may have overheard the parents tell their son about God; indeed, later in life the son may well explain to another person his reason for believing in God ("My parents told me so, and I believed them"), but this will not necessarily convince the other person that God exists (and should not).

In my opinion, a great many beliefs that individuals hold rest on private evidence. This, for me, is the full unpacking of the fact that people do not always follow Russell's Principle. They *do* always follow the amended version (no one believes anything he is not convinced of, something for which he does not believe he has good reasons) ; but people do not always follow Russell's Principle if public evidence alone is what is meant (as Russell clearly must have meant in stating his Principle).

The term *private* has many connotations in contemporary philosophy, so perhaps I should note that I am not saying that evidence can be *logically* private in the sense in which some philosophers have maintained that awareness of sense-data is private. I cannot experience your sense-data, but normally (i.e., outside of ineffable experiences) nothing prevents you from explaining to me your private reasons for believing a proposition. The evidence is private (to you) only in the sense that it is convincing to you while it need not be convincing to me and would not be convincing to the majority of rational persons.

The distinction between public and private evidence will be taken up again later in this study. I shall use the notion of private reasons for belief to describe the epistemological nature of religious faith, and I shall consider what justification there is, if any, for the use of private evidence in evidence-situations. That is, in the light of the questions that can be raised by the philosophical and the religious skeptic, I shall ask if a person is ever justified in allowing his beliefs to be influenced by private evidence.

I wish to make the point that the distinction between public and private reasons for belief is not something I have arbitrarily invented. I should maintain that the distinction is descriptive of the behavior of people in evidence-situations. For we have seen that in evidence-situations: (1) we all tacitly accept Russell's Principle; we wish to condemn as irrational those beliefs which are not based on evidence and praise as rational those which are; (2) on one interpretation of the Principle we constantly break it, that is, we allow factors like prejudices, emotions, biases, and the like to influence our beliefs; (3) yet, on another interpretation, we never break it, that is, we never believe anything for which we do not think that we have adequate evidence. For me, the distinction between public and private evidence is what follows from these facts.

It is simply undeniable that people do believe propositions that others will claim—and indeed that they themselves may admit—are not adequately supported by evidence. But such people will also typically wish to insist that they have reasons —good reasons—for their beliefs. There are perhaps other ways of explaining this fact than appealing to a notion of private evidence. Pascal, for example, once said, "The heart has its reasons that reason does not know."[4] I could have chosen here to speak of "reasons of the heart" rather than "private evidence," but perhaps what Pascal meant by the one does not significantly differ from what I mean by the other. If the reader objects to my using the term *evidence* for anything so subjective as what I am calling *private evidence,* perhaps Pascal's "reasons of the heart" or Kant's "subjectively convincing grounds" will be less objectionable.

Before proceeding to chapter 2, I wish to make two final

points. The first is terminological. Hereafter in this essay where I use the term *evidence* it should be noted that it is always *public evidence* that is meant. I feel safe in adopting this procedure because ordinary uses of the term *evidence* invariably refer to what I am calling public evidence. Where in context the public/private distinction is important, I will use the full terms *public evidence* and *private evidence*.

Second, the perceptive reader will have noticed that there is something of an epistemological circle in this chapter. To the question "How can I tell if evidence for a proposition is good evidence?" I have answered that it is ultimately the consensus of rational persons (i.e., persons who have rational beliefs) that decides. But to the question "How can I tell if a given belief is a rational belief?" I have answered that a rational belief is one that is based on good evidence. I do not find this circularity embarrassing; I simply believe that the epistemic facts are as I have stated them. (Perhaps it is not unlike this circularity: a logical person is one whose thought is consistent with the laws and rules of logic; the laws and rules of logic are authoritative because they agree with the intuitions of logical persons.)

To avoid this circularity, one might attempt to define good evidence in terms of *experience*: e.g., if I claim to have adequate evidence for the proposition "Kucheman owns dogs," this claim will be true, for example, if I have actually seen Kucheman's dogs. If I claim to have adequate evidence for the proposition "Smith was born in What Cheer," this will be true not because I saw Smith born in What Cheer (which I did not) but because the evidence upon which my belief is based (what Smith tells me, what I read in his biography, etc.) is itself ultimately based on someone's actual experience (e.g., that of his mother and father). This sort of maneuver is fine and I have no objection to it as a preliminary way of defining good evidence. But since people interpret their experiences differently, and since it is often difficult to tell whether or not a belief is based on actual experience, I must hold that the final criterion of good evidence is, as I have claimed, what the majority of rational persons hold to be good evidence. Ultimately, I believe, the circularity is unavoidable.

NOTES

1. Bertrand Russell, *A History of Western Philosophy* (New York: Simon and Schuster, 1945), p. 816. Russell is of course not the only philosopher to have formulated this principle. For example, John Locke recommends "not entertaining any proposition with greater assurance than the proofs it is built upon will warrant." *An Essay Concerning Human Understanding,* ed. Alexander C. Fraser, 2 vols. (Oxford: The Clarendon Press, 1894), bk. 4, chap. 19, §1. David Hume says that "a wise man . . . proportions his belief to the evidence." *An Enquiry Concerning Human Understanding* (La Salle, Ill.: The Open Court Publishing Company, 1946), p. 116. W. K. Clifford says, "It is wrong always, everywhere, and for anyone to believe anything upon insufficient evidence." *Lectures and Essays,* ed. Leslie Stephens and Frederick Pollack (New York: Macmillan and Company, 1901), 2:186. P. F. Strawson says, "It is an analytic proposition that it is reasonable to have a degree of belief in a statement which is proportional to the strength of the evidence in its favor." *Introduction to Logical Theory* (London: Methuen and Company, 1952), p. 256.

2. Robert J. Fogelin, *Evidence and Meaning* (London: Routledge and Kegan Paul, 1967), p. 78.

3. Immanuel Kant, *Critique of Pure Reason,* trans. Norman Kemp Smith (New York: St. Martin's Press, 1965), pp. 645–52.

4. Pascal, *Pascal's Pensées* (New York: E. P. Dutton & Co., 1958), p. 78.

2

Knowledge and General Skepticism

There are certain things that we know and certain things that we do not know. Or, at least, so we are used to thinking. For example, I feel perfectly confident in claiming to know that I am now holding a pen in my hand; and I am also perfectly sure that I do not know how many runners finished last year's Boston Marathon.

Let us call a *knowledge-claim* any claim by any person to know a particular statement. Clearly, the knowledge-claims we encounter in the course of a lifetime are exceedingly numerous and diverse.

(1) The sphere I am observing is a baseball.
(2) San Francisco is north of Los Angeles.
(3) $5 \times 7 = 35$.
(4) The sun will rise tomorrow.
(5) Lincoln was the sixteenth president of the United States.
(6) I had dinner at a friend's house last night.
(7) The Mona Lisa is a beautiful painting.
(8) Murder is morally wrong.
(9) God exists.

What impresses us about this list, and indeed about the set of all knowledge-claims, is its great variety. Proposition (1) is concerned with perception; (2) is about an empirical or scientifically discoverable fact; (3) states a mathematical truth; (4) concerns the future; (5) concerns a historical fact; (6) is a claim based upon memory; (7) is an aesthetic value judgment; (8) is a moral value judgment; and (9) is a theological statement.

One of the major problems of epistemology is the question of the criteria of knowledge. The question is this: what are the conditions that must be satisfied before I can legitimately claim to know p, where p is any proposition? What I will call the traditional approach to the question was established for later philosophy by Plato in the *Theatetus,* where he asked, What is it which when added to true belief creates knowledge? This approach has been abandoned as fruitless by some contemporary philosophers, but it will be helpful to outline the usual course of the argument.

(1)   One condition that obviously must be satisfied before I can legitimately be said to know p is that I must believe p. This is because such sentences as "I know p but I do not believe p" are nonsensical. But belief is clearly not sufficient in itself to establish knowledge, for people believe many things that they do not know. For example, I believe that it will rain in Los Angeles sometime in December of next year, but I hardly know this.

(2)   Indeed, people often believe things that are not true, for example, many people believed after 1960 that Richard Nixon would never be elected President. This leads us to the second condition. If I know p, then it must be the case that p is true. This is because such sentences as "I know p but not-p" are nonsensical; for example, "Jones knows it is raining but it is not raining." Conditions (1) and (2) together mean that I must have true belief that p before I can know p, but is true belief sufficient in itself to constitute knowledge? Apparently not, for there seem to be many cases where people believe true statements without knowing them.

For example, let us suppose that a superstitious person has his path crossed by a black cat and then believes that some disaster will befall him. And suppose further that a disaster does occur—say he falls and breaks an arm a few minutes later. If all this did occur, would it be true to say that he *knew* that a disaster would befall him? We would be inclined to say no. Or a gambler might firmly believe that a certain number will turn up next on a roulette wheel and it might turn up next, but if it did, would it be correct to say that he knew it? Again, we would be inclined to say no (unless the wheel was rigged and he had been told what it was going to do). And the reason we would be inclined to deny that true belief is knowledge is that it is possible to be correct by sheer luck rather than by knowledge.

(3)   So some third criterion is needed, and this is where philosophers have encountered the most serious difficulties. One common suggestion is that the third criterion is adequate evidence. That is, the suggestion is that I can legitimately be said to know p when (1) I believe p, (2) p is true, and (3) I have adequate evidence for p. This approach takes its cue from the conclusion of the last paragraph that knowledge is not luckily believing what is true. For example, if I say "I know that all tigers have stripes, because yesterday I saw a striped tiger in the zoo," we would doubt that this true belief constitutes knowledge, for seeing one tiger is inadequate evidence to substantiate a claim about all tigers. Similarly we would regard as ill-founded the claim of a person who says "I know that Antonius Pius was a Roman Emperor, because the name has an imperial ring to it."

Thus, according to this form of the traditional analysis of knowledge, I can legitimately be said to know p when I have a true belief that p and have adequate evidence that p. But a refinement is necessary here. Not only must I "have" adequate evidence that p: my belief that p must be based on the adequate evidence that I have. This is to rule out a person's being aware of adequate evidence that p but believing p for some other (inadequate) reason. For example, in September 1964 a person may have correctly believed that Lyndon Johnson would win the ensuing presidential election, and he may have been aware of adequate evidence for this (unanimous opinion of the polls and political experts that

Johnson would win decisively, etc.) , but he may have held this belief not because of the adequate evidence but because of what he saw in his tea leaves.

There is another problem as well. Suppose there is a person Smith who is consistently able to predict the results of horse races. Observers cannot discover any method that Smith uses in arriving at his predictions, and Smith himself (with apparent sincerity) claims that he is ignorant of how he comes to make the predictions that he makes. Nevertheless, he is consistently correct, time and again. We cannot say that Smith's predictions are based on adequate evidence: they do not appear to be based on evidence at all. Yet surely there would come a time after noticing his string of successes when we would be prepared to grant: "He *knows* which horse is going to win." Some philosophers have concluded from this factually doubtful but logically possible event that the third criterion should not be "I have adequate evidence for p," but rather "I have the right to be sure that p." For we cannot talk about any evidence, adequate or otherwise, that Smith's predictions are based upon, but we can talk about his having the right to be sure.

But there is an even more serious difficulty in this account of the conditions of knowledge—one that was noticed first by Plato. It is that there is an apparent circularity in this definition of knowledge; that is, this account of knowledge presupposes knowledge. For surely my true belief that p cannot count as knowledge unless I *know* that the evidence is adequate (or alternatively unless I *know* that I have the right to be sure) . Otherwise, the evidence does not appear strong enough to support a claim to know. If I correctly believed in September 1964 that Lyndon Johnson would win the next presidential election, and if this belief was based on adequate evidence, but if I did not then know that the evidence was adequate, surely I could not legitimately have claimed to know that Johnson would win the election. Or if I correctly believe that today is June 28, and if this belief is based on the adequate evidence that yesterday a friend correctly said to me "Today is June 27," but if I do not know that my friend's statement was true, surely I cannot legitimately claim to know that "today is June 28." But however the point is made, the upshot is that the concept of adequate evidence presupposes just what we are trying to define by making use of it, namely, knowledge. That is, we are defining knowledge by reference to having adequate evidence (or having the right to be sure), which is defined by reference to having knowledge.

But the most serious difficulty of all in stating the conditions of knowledge is the notorious "Gettier problem."[1] What Gettier does is introduce counterexamples to the traditional analysis of knowledge, the intuitive gist of which appears to be this: in the case of any given knowledge-claim, it is possible that the purported knower may have a belief that is true only because of circumstances of which he is entirely ignorant; that is, unluckily for him, the strong evidence that is available to him in support of his knowledge-claim is misleading in some way.

Let us suppose that Jones has a true belief that his friend Smith owns a Ford. Suppose further that Jones's true belief is based on adequate evidence (Smith has always owned Fords, Jones rode in Smith's latest Ford only yesterday, etc.). Then by ordinary logic, "Smith owns a Ford" entails "Smith owns a Ford or Brown (another friend of Jones) is in Barcelona." Now suppose that in spite of Jones's evidence, Smith does *not* own a Ford (today he traded his Ford in on a Fiat). And suppose further that, quite unbeknownst to Jones, Brown *is* in Barcelona. It appears, then, that "Smith owns a Ford or Brown is in Barcelona" is (1) believed by Jones (a rational person, he knows it is entailed by "Smith owns a Ford"), (2) true, and (3) based on adequate evidence. Yet surely we do not want to say that Jones *knows* this proposition.

Gettier's counter-examples appear to undermine the traditional analysis of knowledge. Thus they have stimulated an enormous literature in the philosophical journals, most of it devoted to repairing or amending it in some way. It is not part of my program in this study to join in the attempt to solve Gettier's problem. I merely wish to point out one way in which his problem seems to give weight to philosophical skepticism: a Gettier type of counterexample seems to exist for any knowledge-claim whatsoever about things outside the consciousness of the knower. That is, in the case of any "external" fact we claim to know, our belief may be true only because of sheer luck rather than knowledge.

We can again see how the traditional analysis raises the specter of skepticism if we take a slightly different approach toward the third criterion. Let us now say that Jones knows that p if and only if:

(10)   Jones believes p
(11)   p is true
(12)   Jones can answer all objections to p.

The difficulty is that (12) is ambiguous. What sorts of objections are meant here? Must Jones answer all the logically possible objections that might be raised against p or just what we might call the "current objections," that is, those of which Jones is (or, alternatively, should be) aware of? Or again, must he answer only those objections which are themselves based on (at least some) evidence (let us call these *real objections*), or must he also be able to answer the sorts of objections that a Cartesian methodical doubter might raise (let us call these *Cartesian objections*)? (For example, if p is "I had lunch with Adams yesterday," a real objection might be, "But Adams told me he skipped lunch yesterday," while a Cartesian objection might be, "But how can you be sure you did not merely dream that you had lunch with Adams yesterday?").

There seem, then, to be four significant versions of (12):

(12a)   Jones can answer all current real objections to p
(12b)   Jones can answer all current real and Cartesian objections to p

(12c) Jones can answer all possible real objections to p
(12d) Jones can answer all possible real and Cartesian objections to p.

Which interpretation of (12) should we accept? Unfortunately, there appear to be serious difficulties connected with each. Versions (12c) and (12d) both appear to lead to skepticism: how could Jones ever be sure that he had answered all the *logically possible* objections to p (of either sort)? Version (12b) also leads to skepticism in that some Cartesian objections, once we allow them to be raised, are clearly unanswerable. How could Jones ever rule out the possibility that he merely dreamed that he had had lunch with Adams yesterday? Or how could he prove that it was really Adams with whom he had lunch and not a Martian spy cleverly disguised as Adams?

Thus (12a), the weakest of the four, appears to be the only interpretation that makes knowledge possible. But does it? We now have this claim: Jones knows that p if and only if

(10) Jones believes p
(11) p is true
(12a) Jones can answer all current real objections to p.

There are three problems here. First, the skeptic will want to know our reason for accepting (12a). Do we *know* that it is the true third condition of knowledge? Can we meet all the current real objections to p where p is "(12a) is the third condition of knowledge"? Surely, the skeptic might claim, our acceptance of (12a) is question-begging against skepticism if it is accepted merely because it alone appears to support the claim that we do indeed know. And if this is not our reason for accepting (12a), and if we can give no evidence in its favor, then our acceptance of (12a) must be based merely on faith.

Second, acceptance of the (10), (11), and (12a) version of the traditional analysis of knowledge leaves open the possibility of our old bugaboo that Jones truly believes p out of luck rather than knowledge. I am not so much thinking of Gettier here, though Gettier types of counterexample can easily be raised against this version of the traditional analysis too. I am thinking of the possibility that there is a strong, noncurrent objection to p that Jones cannot answer. Since (11) still holds (strong objections can be raised against truths), Jones's belief in p is still a true belief. But it seems an open question whether he actually knows. Suppose that p is "Today is April 3." And suppose Jones holds this true belief because yesterday Smith told him "Today is April 2." Finally, suppose Jones can answer all the real objections to p except this one: "Yesterday was really April 1, and Smith told Jones it was April 2 only as an April Fool's joke." Does Jones really know?

And, third, the old circularity difficulty comes up again with a vengeance: (12a) will apparently do the job of an adequate third condition of knowledge only if it is *known* that Jones can answer all current real objections to p. Thus we are again presupposing knowledge in order to explain knowledge.

Despite these and other difficulties, the traditional analysis of knowledge has a strong hold on philosophers, and perhaps most are inclined to defend versions of it. And it does seem that *some* form of the third criterion is needed, lest knowledge reduce to true belief, which violates some of our deepest intuitions about knowledge. I do not propose to discuss the matter further at this point; my aim has been to show some of the serious difficulties involved in saying just what knowledge is.

It will have been noticed that I have been referring in the preceding paragraphs to skepticism. As I noted at the outset of this chapter, we are used to assuming that we do indeed know certain things. We might differ about which propositions are actually known and by whom, but most of us are prepared to grant that at least some knowledge-claims are justified. Let us call anyone who believes that at least some things can be known a "nonskeptic."

I say "most of us" because there is one sort of philosopher

who is not willing to grant this: the skeptic. There are two sorts of skeptics we shall be concerned with in this essay, the philosophical or general skeptic and the religious skeptic. The philosophical skeptic is the person who denies or doubts that any proposition can be known; the religious skeptic is the person who may admit that some things can be known but who denies that there is ever any rational justification for accepting religious propositions. For the present, I am concerned with the philosophical skeptic; later I will turn to the religious skeptic.

A casual look at the literature in the history of philosophy might make one think that philosophical skeptics abound. Many epistemologists attack the arguments of the philosophical skeptic with an energy that suggests a deep-seated conviction that there are skeptics hiding under every rock and that they must be refuted. But in actuality there have been few philosophical skeptics. Perhaps one of the reasons for this is that the most obvious form of philosophical skepticism is self-contradictory. The skeptic who says "Nothing can be known" is clearly making a knowledge-claim; that is, he is claiming to know that "nothing can be known." There are, however, much more sophisticated versions of skepticism than this.

Suppose a general skeptic approaches us with his doubt that anything can be known. He does not claim to know that nothing can be known; he just doubts that any knowledge-claim can be substantiated. To refute him, if that is what we want to do, we must of course show him that certain things can be known. That is, to refute such a skeptic it must not merely be true that we do know things; we must be able to *show* or prove that we do. We must not only know; we must know that we know. This is required by the logic of the situation. But unfortunately, as we shall see, this plays into the skeptic's hands; he is able to exploit this requirement for his own purposes.

Let us look at the arguments of the Hellenistic philosopher Sextus Empiricus (ca. A.D. 160–210). Apparently a Greek physician, Sextus was the last major figure in the long history of the Greek and Roman Skeptical school of philosophy that began with Pyrrho (ca. 360–275 B.C.). Sextus wrote several philosophical treatises, some of which are lost, but he was more a historian or cataloguer of skeptical arguments than an original thinker. Nevertheless, his views are to be taken seriously, because they illustrate both the lines that a philosophical skeptic is likely to take and the difficulties that exist for his viewpoint.

Sextus is not the sort of skeptic who makes the self-defeating claim "Nothing can be known." He makes a distinction between *apparent* or *evident* things and nonapparent or non-evident things. Sextus is prepared to admit that apparent things can be known, for example, such sentences as "I am now perceiving a yellow patch," "I am now thinking about the weather." But beyond what later philosophers would call *that of which we are immediately aware*, Sextus denies that truth can ever be known.

The reason for this is that on any nonevident question, a good case can be made in favor of both sides. For every argument in favor of a proposition p, there seems (at least to Sextus) to be an argument of equal strength against p. Opposing arguments tend simply to cancel each other out and we cannot decide which conclusion to accept. But again, Sextus wishes to avoid making knowledge-claims, even the knowledge-claim "The arguments for and against any proposition are always equal." He instead retires to the level of apparent things and says, "The arguments *seem* to me equal in force." That is, he is not speaking about the actual soundness or unsoundness of opposing arguments but about his own state of mind when he encounters them. So he does not dogmatically claim that knowledge is in principle impossible, but rather that it seems to him at present that certainty cannot be obtained on nonevident things.[2]

Thus it does not surprise us that Sextus shows great skill in juxtaposing opposing arguments on all sorts of nonevident questions. He spends page after page in doing so—listing arguments on both sides of nonevident questions, the obvious implication being that neither side can be shown to be stronger. If no counter-arguments to a knowledge-claim are immediately apparent, the skeptic (Sextus tells us) will actively seek such arguments and, once they are found, will state them as strongly as possible. If weak arguments will do, they too can be used. As a last resort the skeptic might even use the expedient of saying: "Some day someone might think of a strong argument against yours, just as your argument was unknown before its discovery; so it is impossible to tell which side to accept."[3]

This pose strikes us as slightly contrived. We want to object that Sextus has apparently decided a priori that we can never tell what to believe on nonapparent matters. But here Sextus introduces an important consideration: his denial that there is a "criterion" of truth. A criterion of truth is a judge that evaluates knowledge-claims, a scale on which to weigh them, a sign that a true proposition is before us, like, say, a bell that rings whenever a true proposition is encountered.[4] Sextus argues that no such infallible criterion exists, and thus his point is not that it is in fact difficult to evaluate arguments but rather in principle impossible. If there are no scales, how can we judge the weightiness of arguments?

No criterion can exist because for any purported criterion we would need another criterion to tell whether or not *it* is genuine, and a criterion for that criterion, and so on. (Without a second criterion, how would we ever know for sure that the truth bell is ringing? What if one person claims and another person denies that it is ringing?) That is, any purported criterion used to evaluate the nonapparent can be challenged simply by asking whether or not *it* is apparent. Again, however, Sextus (usually) backs away from making a knowledge-claim: it is not "It is known that no criterion exists" but rather "No known criterion exists." That is, having taken up and disposed of all suggested criteria (as he does in detail in both *Against the Logicians* and *Outlines of Pyrrhonism*[5]), he concludes that none of the suggested criteria suffices. Thus, since we have no acceptable criterion, disagreements have no authoritative way of being settled. In matters of debate about nonevident questions, one person's case is as good as his opponent's, and we cannot know whose is true.

Since one of the suggested criteria rejected by Sextus is reason, he mounts a strong attack on the concept of *proof*. He defines proof as a conclusive and true argument with a nonevident conclusion that is discovered through the power of the premises.[6] But thus defined, proof cannot be had, and for two principal reasons. The first reason is that there is no criterion of truth: "A proof cannot be sound without the preexistence of a true criterion, and a criterion cannot be true either without prior confirmations of the proof. And so both the criterion and the proof fall into circular argument, in which both are found to be untrustworthy."[7] In other words, the concept of proof is nonevident, and thus to be acceptable must either (1) be proved by reference to itself, which is circular reasoning, or (2) be proved by reference to something else, which means that proof is not really proof but the "something else" is. Furthermore, since there is no criterion of truth, there is no universally accepted "something else" that would suffice to prove a proof. And even if there were, that "something else" would itself have to be proved, and the proof of the "something else" would have to be proved, et cetera, ad infinitum.

Second, proof is nonexistent because there are always doubts about the factual truth of the premises of any proof. Every proof, Sextus says, contains an opinion in the premises that itself needs to be factually substantiated before the proof will work. But since people disagree in their opinions and since no criterion exists by which to establish one person's view over another's, proof is nonexistent.[8] (I shall note later that despite this theoretical demonstration of the non-existence of proof, Sextus *in practice* quite often tries to prove things.)

What, then, must the philosopher do? The answer is obvious, according to Sextus. The truth is unknowable; we cannot know how things really are, but only how they appear to us. Thus on all nonevident matters, all we can do is adopt the state of "suspension of judgment," which Sextus defines as "cessation of the thought processes in consequence of which we neither deny nor affirm anything."[9] This is not a categorical denial of the possibility of knowledge: in the final analysis, Sextus does not even claim that his own skeptical statements are true. He simply says, "My state of mind at the present is such that I make no dogmatic affirmation or denial of anything falling under the present investigation."[10] So Sextus wants us to understand him as asserting nothing; skepticism is (1) merely a report of present impressions and (2) suspension of judgment on nonevident things. It is a laxative that in the end washes everything from the body, even itself.

Sextus concludes with the comforting thought that skepticism is the only path to true mental tranquillity. The non-skeptic can never achieve an undisturbed state of mind, for he is always seeking and failing to find adequate grounds for certainty on nonevident questions. He always ends in frustration. This is the chief practical value of skepticism: it removes all dogmatic concerns and permits us to live a happy, unperturbed life, following our natural instincts and the customs and laws of the society in which we live.

As noted, Sextus usually carefully guards against making the self-contradictory claim that nothing can be known. What he tries to do is simply exhibit for us the various arguments on both sides of any knowledge-claim, the implication being that we ought to suspend judgment as he has done. But it may be that he is guilty of a related error, or indeed a more subtle version of this same error, and it will be instructive for us to look into it.

One of the things we find most puzzling in Sextus is his rejection of proof. For it seems obvious that Sextus is using proof to destroy proof—after all, he does propose *arguments* against the concept of proof—and indeed this was one of the standard objections to ancient skepticism. The usual skeptical reply to this was to appeal to the metaphor of a ladder which, once ascended, is no longer needed and can be discarded. But perhaps the matter is more serious than this. If the ladder can be discarded (proof can be shown to be unattainable) after having first been used (after things have been successfully proved), do we not have grounds for doubting that the first use of the ladder was indeed successful? And perhaps Sextus's use of the notion of proof shows that he is in fact tacitly using some criterion of truth.

For example, if there were no criterion of truth, we wonder how Sextus could categorize and label arguments as he does. How could he call arguments *weighty, extremely ludicrous, in accord with the facts, false, reasonable, contrary to reason,* or *logical*[11] unless he is using some criterion by which to evaluate them? Furthermore, if there is no criterion (and thus no proof), how is it that Sextus constantly claims to have "proved" things?[12]

> Well then, let us take this as proof that man is incapable of forming a ready conception of himself.

> But it is also possible to prove . . . that all things are relative.

> These arguments, then, should be enough to show that man is unable to perceive either the senses by means of the body, or . . . the body by means of the senses.

It seems that Sextus makes liberal practical use of the concept of proof (and thus, by his own argument, of some criterion), all the while claiming that neither criterion nor proof exists.

It is true that the notion of *proof* and the notion of *truth* belong in different logical realms, so to speak. *Proof* belongs in the realm of deductive logic and *truth* in the realm of empirical claims. So Sextus might argue that his use of proof does not commit him to the existence of any criterion of truth. He might claim that the distinction between validity and invalidity is something that emerges from a decision to play a game by certain rules. Thus in the argument

(13)   If p then q or r or s
(14)   Not q and not r and not s
(15)   Therefore, not p

no criterion of truth is being used; we have merely agreed to play by certain rules (de Morgan and *modus tollens*). In other words, we do not claim to have given a true description of any empirical object in the world.

This may be true, but my point is just that Sextus does have a guide to what can and cannot be believed, and that is logic. Any argument that in any way violates the canons of logic Sextus rejects, and Sextus accepts a great many arguments that show that other arguments violate the canons of logic. Again, Sextus can admit that he accepts the law of noncontradiction and other logical laws and still deny that this provides a criterion by which to discover empirical truths. But it does seem that the laws of logic perform the job of a criterion for Sextus, that is, they serve as standards by which to judge (at least certain sorts of) knowledge-claims. Furthermore, Sextus himself says that there can be no proof without a criterion; since he successfully proves things he must be using a criterion. Thus Sextus is inconsistent in basing so much of his philosophical method on logic while denying that reason or logic (or anything else) is a criterion of truth. In other words, Sextus ought openly to have admitted his acceptance of logical laws and ought to have made some attempt to see in what way such an admission would have qualified his skepticism.

Sextus might reply to this (1) that the laws of logic only *seem* acceptable to him and that he is making no knowledge-claim about them, or (2) that they seem acceptable to the nonskeptic and that he is only attempting to refute the non-skeptic on his own ground. But the problem with this is that Sextus does accept and even explicitly state laws of logic in several places:[13]

But of course conflicting things cannot be true.

But it is impossible that the same thing should both exist and not exist, and be both true and false.

It is absurd to say that the same thing both is and is not.

. . . the same thing will be other than itself (both cause and effect simultaneously) ; and both these conclusions are illogical.

If it only seems to Sextus that the laws are sound, or if he is only "accepting" the laws in order to refute the nonskeptic on his own ground, Sextus's confident use of the laws as a club to beat other philosophers over the head is at the very least puzzling. It is true that you cannot refute a person who merely speaks about his own state of mind. But if Sextus's argument amounts merely to the claim that what he says in his works seems to him sound, why cannot a nonskeptic reply that it seems to him unsound? In point of fact, while there are places where Sextus takes pains to warn that he is speaking only about his personal feelings at a given point in time, there are many other places where he seems to be doing much more than this: he seems, that is, to be attempting to make true statements. For example, he never seems to doubt the nonevident statement "Other people have beliefs," for if he refused to accept *this* proposition there would be nothing for him to refute. Of course there is nothing to prevent Sextus from placing his entire corpus of writings in brackets and, as it were, saying of the bracketed material: "In all of this material I make no knowledge-claims; my statements are only expressions of my feelings at various points in time." But he pays a price if he does this: his argument will have no logical force against the nonskeptic who says, "Well and good, but my feelings are different."

Indeed, when Sextus attempts to reply to criticisms that nonskeptics have made against skepticism, he seems to abandon any pose of suspension of judgment or "it just seems so to me." Instead, he begins to argue for his own position: he tries to show, that is, that arguments *are* balanced, that there is *no* criterion, and that we *should* suspend judgment. For example, in *Against the Logicians* Sextus states the criticism noted earlier: that skeptics use proof to disprove proof and thus establish it in their attempt to deny it. But instead of taking this argument (together with conflicting arguments in favor of skepticism) as a reason for suspending judgment on the question of the acceptability of skepticism, he proceeds to attempt to *answer* the objection (with the metaphor of the no-longer-needed ladder). Thus, when pressed by antiskeptical arguments, Sextus does not suspend judgment on their validity but attempts to reach a conclusion about them. And how can one argue for his own (or any other) position if there is no criterion by which to judge the relative merits of arguments?

If Sextus is inconsistent in his attempt to state his form of skepticism, this is not necessarily to say that general skepticism is inherently inconsistent and that the errors cannot be repaired. In fact, I believe it is quite possible to invent a brand of general skepticism that is immune to the sorts of criticism that can be made against Sextus.

I propose now to sketch one such skeptical position, a view I will call *adequate skepticism*. It is a skepticism that is in the spirit of Sextus and the Greek Skeptical school he represents, and I believe that it accomplishes what he was trying to accomplish. What the adequate skeptic does is make no statements of his own and raise no criticisms of the statements of others: he simply shows, by the questions he asks, that no knowledge-claim can be substantiated, and that there is no good reason for believing any proposition.

The strategy of the adequate skeptic is to reduce the nonskeptic to an infinite regress. The nonskeptic says "I know p." To this, the adequate skeptic asks, "How do you know p; i.e., can you substantiate your knowledge-claim, e.g., by showing that it is based on adequate evidence?" If he is to defend himself, the nonskeptic must now reply in some such form as, "The ground for my acceptance of p is q." But of course the adequate skeptic will then reply: "How do you know q?" This is what the adequate skeptic will always ask whenever the nonskeptic attempts to produce reasons for belief. There are an infinite number of such questions the adequate skeptic can ask, and since (as we saw earlier) all knowledge-claims must be based on adequate evidence, the nonskeptic can never show that his acceptance of p is based on adequate evidence or that he has the right to be certain of p. That is, he can never show that he knows p.

What is clearly needed against the adequate skeptic is some stopping place, some statement of the form, "My ground for r is just r itself and r needs no evidence." And this is precisely why very many philosophers have attempted to combat the skeptic by searching for something that can be incorrigibly known, that is, some statement whose truth cannot be doubted. That is, they have tried to discover something that can be immediately or intuitively known, something that is directly evident and for which there is no need to offer evidence. And once discovered, the attempt is made to justify knowledge-claims by leading them back, step-by-step, to that which is directly evident.

Philosophers have located incorrigibles in two main places. Some have claimed that necessary truths such as "2 + 2 = 4" or "Two straight lines do not enclose an area" are self-evident and that knowledge-claims can be substantiated by reference to them. Others have located incorrigibles in the realm of direct sensory experience. They have looked to private contingent statements like "I now see a blue patch," "I now feel pain" (what Sextus called the realm of "evident things"). But confronted with either sort of incorrigible, the adequate skeptic will ask whether it is possible to justify the knowledge-claim, "Corrigible knowledge-claims can be incorrigibly connected to the incorrigible." Unfortunately, there seems no way to justify any move from the corrigible to the incorrigible, for example, by showing that corrigible statements are incorrigibly derivable from incorrigible statements or that incorrigible statements can constitute incorrigibly conclusive reasons for accepting corrigible statements.

But what if someone objects as follows: "Who says that if I know p and believe p on the (adequate) grounds of q that I must know q too? Does not this high standard of knowledge conflict with the claim that standards of adequacy are ultimately determined by consensus? For surely the consensus of rational people might decide that it is not necessary to know q in order to know p."

The answer to this is that consensus determines when evidence for a given hypothesis is adequate, but not whether or not q must be known if p is to be known. This conclusion is reached by argument, not by consensus. Suppose I claim to know that my family and I have been invited to a picnic to be held next week, and suppose my evidence for this knowledge-claim is my belief that my wife told me that she received a phone call inviting us. Surely I do not *know* that we have been invited to a picnic to be held next week (1) if it is false that my wife told me that she received a phone call inviting us (I misunderstood my wife), or (2) if I have inadequate evidence that my wife told me that she received a phone call inviting us (sick with fever, I have been delirious all day and am not sure whether my wife's telling about the picnic was real or imagined).

Therefore there are forms of skepticism that are inconsistent, but adequate skepticism, since it entails no position, is consistent. The adequate skeptic merely doubts that any knowledge-claim can be substantiated. He makes no statements; he merely shows, instance by instance, that the statements of others are not really known. Note that the adequate skeptic does not claim to know that knowledge is impossible. He simply asks to be shown an example of justified knowledge-claim; he can hardly be criticized if none of the candidates measure up to the needed standards of adequacy.

NOTES

1. See Edmund L. Gettier, "Is Justified True Belief Knowledge?," *Analysis* 23 (1963): 121–23.

2. Philp P. Hallie, *Scepticism, Man, and God: Selections From the Major Writings of Sextus Empiricus* (Middletown, Conn.: Wesleyan University Press, 1964), pp. 82–84, 86–87.

3. Ibid., p. 43; cf. p. 128.

4. Sextus explains what he means by the term *criterion* in *Outlines of Pyrrhonism,* trans. R. G. Bury (Cambridge, Mass.: Harvard University Press, 1933), p. 161, and in *Against The Logicians,* trans. R. G. Bury (Cambridge, Mass.: Harvard University Press, 1935), pp. 17–19.

5. Hallie, *Skepticism,* pp. 140–48; Sextus, *Outlines,* pp. 161–203.

6. Sextus, *Against the Logicians,* p. 403.

7. Hallie, *Skepticism,* pp. 62–63; cf. p. 141.

8. Sextus, *Against the Logicians,* pp. 411, 433, 247–49.

9. Hallie, *Skepticism,* p. 34.

10. Ibid., p. 83; cf. p. 31.

11. Hallie, *Skepticism,* pp. 128, 186, 192, 143, 45, 156, 56.

12. Ibid., pp. 134, 67, 139.

13. Sextus, *Against the Logicians,* pp. 253, 263; Hallie, *Skepticism,* p. 123. *Against the Logicians,* p. 207.

3

A Pragmatic Reply to Skepticism

One odd but undeniable fact about adequate skepticism is that it would be difficult, indeed impossible, to live by such a position. Of course, as noted, since the adequate skeptic makes no statements, his is not truly a position and could be described as the absence of a position about any nonevident thing. But still, it seems that a person who sincerely doubts that any knowledge-claim can be substantiated, that is, a person who is unwilling to affirm that anything nonevident is known, would have no recourse but either (1) to deny his philosophy by accepting propositions like "Food nourishes," "Fire burns," "Water quenches thirst," and so on, or else (2) to live by his philosophy and merely lie down and die.

"But surely we can live by probability rather than knowledge," a defender of adequate skepticism might reply at this point; "we don't have to know or even claim to know that fire burns in order to avoid being burned: we just have to accept that the proposition 'Fire burns' is *probably* true." But the answer to this is that a knowledge-claim is being made here after all: the knowledge-claim "It is probable that fire burns."

"But surely we can live by belief rather than knowledge," another defender of adequate skepticism might reply; "we don't have to know or even claim to know that fire burns in order to avoid being burned: we just have to *believe* that fire burns." No doubt there is truth here. A person can hold beliefs and even act on those beliefs without claiming that the propositions believed are known. But such a person will not be a Sextus type of skeptic, for he does not suspend judgment; he makes affirmations and denials about non-evident things. He commits himself to the truth of such propositions as "Fire burns" with no less energy and intensity than does the nonskeptic. Since it is true that he will never claim to know, possibly there is some legitimate sense in which he can still call himself a skeptic. But he is in truth what might be called a *practical* nonskeptic.

Let us define a "consistent skeptic" as a skeptic who "practices what he preaches," that is, who not only refuses verbally to admit that any nonevident thing can be known but who also lives by this refusal. A consistent skeptic, in short, is a person who lives in such a way as to *show* that he doubts that any nonevident thing can be known.

Philosophers like to believe that the positions they espouse have relevance to real life. But what we notice about skepticism is that there have been no consistent skeptics in the history of philosophy (at least none that we know of). There have been skeptics like Sextus who claim to doubt that any nonevident thing can be known but who go on living as if nonevident things can be known. (Sextus goes to great pains to show that skepticism enhances the ability to live the ordinary life of eating, drinking, conversing, etc. The skeptic, he says, will follow his own natural inclinations without, however, making any knowledge-claims like "Food nourishes.") But if it is the case (as it is often said) that what a person truly believes is revealed more by how he behaves than what he says, does it not follow that the skeptic who eats food whenever he is hungry is committed *in some sense* to the truth of the knowledge-claim "Food nourishes"? If this is true, is it not then the case that such a skeptic is not really so skeptical as he would like us to believe? Is doubt genuine if it fails to affect behavior in any important way? Suppose I claim to be unsure whether or not the sidewalk will support my weight and yet I walk unhesitatingly on it. Am I really in a state of doubt?

Take Cratylus, for example. Cratylus is a figure about whom we know little—he was apparently a teacher of Plato before Plato met Socrates—but he is perhaps the most consistent of the skeptics we read about in the history of philosophy. He apparently believed that communication between one person and another is impossible. All things are in constant flux, he believed, including persons and the meanings of the words they speak. It follows that when Jones says sentence s to Smith, s means one thing, but when Smith hears s, s means something else. So it is said that Cratylus decided to speak and write nothing. He merely wagged his finger in the air when spoken to in order to indicate that he had heard something but that it would be useless to reply.

But even finger-wagging is a form of communication, is it not? We are suspicious that had Cratylus been consistently skeptical he would not have been sure enough of the nonevident knowledge-claim "I just heard sounds emanate from this person in front of me" to wag his finger at all. If the person who spoke the sounds was about to become different from the person who was to observe Cratylus's finger-wagging, indeed if the Cratylus who heard the sounds was about to become different from the Cratylus who was to wag the finger, what was the point of the finger-wagging? Perhaps Cratylus could defend himself here—maybe the finger-wagging only made the finger-wagging Cratylus feel better—but we suspect that there were certain knowledge-claims about nonevident things that in practice Cratylus showed he did not care to doubt.

If philosophy is not relevant to life as it is actually lived by men and women, then it is surely questionable whether it is an enterprise worth engaging in. Thus, if it is true that adequate skepticism is a position that cannot be refuted, it is a scandal to philosophy that it is also a position that cannot consistently be lived. Is it true that adequate skepticism cannot be refuted? I believe so: since the adequate skeptic commits himself to no actual position, he cannot be refuted for the obvious reason that there is nothing to refute. As a position, adequate skepticism is empty. Pointing this out might 'seem to the nonskeptic to be a way of defeating the adequate skeptic, but if so it is a hollow victory, for it does not show that we should not be adequate skeptics.

To lay my cards on the table: I see no way that the adequate skeptic can be refuted. There are no logical difficulties involved in his position; his attitude cannot be shown to be false or inconsistent. But perhaps grounds can be found for the claim that we should not take the questions of the adequate skeptic seriously. These will not be logical or evidential grounds but rather pragmatic grounds. To develop this pragmatic critique or "refutation" of adequate skepticism is the aim of this chapter.

But first let us look at David Hume's views on skepticism, for they have influenced the position I will develop here. First of all, Hume was a firm believer in the relevance of philosophy to life. He says, "Though a philosopher may live remote from business, the genius of philosophy, if carefully cultivated by several, must gradually diffuse itself throughout the whole of society, and bestow a similar correctness on every art and calling."[1]

Nevertheless, Hume committed himself to (a certain sort of) skepticism and considered his skepticism irrefutable. Hume's skepticism was directed against certain claims made by other philosophers. He was not content merely to ask questions; he suggested definite arguments against the claims he criticized. Hume's skepticism is far-reaching and touches upon many beliefs held by nonskeptics. To take an illustrative example, let us look at Hume's argument about knowledge-claims concerning future or otherwise unobserved events.

Suppose I am out of doors on a cold day. I am chilled and decide to come inside. I look forward to the fire in the living room because it will warm me (so I suppose). If I were asked how I know that the fire in the living room will warm me I would answer that it is because all fires I have ever encountered in the past have emitted heat and that whenever I have stood in front of the fireplace in the living room in the past when there was a fire going I have been warmed. At this point Hume would quickly point out that I am presupposing that the future will be like the past (past fires warmed, so future fires will warm). And this is quite right: my argument collapses unless this assumption is true. He then asks, Do we have any evidence that the future will be like the past? If I say that my evidence is just that all past fires have warmed me I have not given any evidence that *future* fires will. If I say that past anticipations that fires would warm me invariably led to past realizations of those anticipations, Hume would say that this merely gives evidence that past futures were like past pasts. My statement does not touch the question whether future futures will be like the past. Hume concludes that we have no evidence that the future will be like the past and never can have any such evidence. Thus there is no rational basis for my view that the fire will warm me.[2]

With these and other arguments Hume attempts to show that we do not really know that God exists, that the external world exists, that the senses are reliable sources of information, that mathematical propositions are true, or that there exists an "I" or "self" that is the locus of personal identity. Hume believed that skeptical arguments destroy any attempt to gain certain knowledge. In the light of his critique, he concludes that nothing is certain: no opinion is more likely than any other; there is no rational basis for our beliefs.[3] Hume even proposes an argument similar to the infinite-regress strategy of the adequate skeptic: there are, he says, an infinite number of critical questions that can be asked about any knowledge-claim, and with each successive question the belief becomes weaker, for each question raises a new possibility that I might have been mistaken in believing p (the knowledge-claim) or q (the evidence for p) or r (the evidence for q), and so forth.[4]

But despite the fact that he believes that the arguments

of the skeptic are irrefutable, Hume goes on to point out that skepticism cannot be accepted either. Skepticism, he says, can be neither refuted nor believed: skeptical arguments "admit of no answer and produce no conviction."[5]

> For here is the chief and most confounding objection to *excessive* scepticism, that no durable good can result from it. . . . [The skeptic] must acknowledge, if he will acknowledge anything, that all human life must perish, were his principles universally and steadily to prevail. All discourse, all action would immediately cease; and men remain in a total lethargy, till the necessities of nature, unsatisfied, put an end to their miserable existence.[6]

Skeptical arguments are well and good, says Hume, but when it comes to the practical problems of living, we are bound to hold beliefs like "Food nourishes," "Fire burns," et cetera. Human nature breaks the force of skeptical arguments and insures that they will have little influence on us. We then have no choice but to yield to the impulses of our natures; beliefs are unavoidable. Nature in this way protects us; our beliefs allow us to live. We would perish if we did not hold them, for skepticism is incompatible with those beliefs we must hold in order to live.

There are, Hume says, no total skeptics: "Whoever has taken the pains to refute the cavils of this total skepticism, has really disputed without an antagonist."[7] Hume calls the kind of skepticism he accepts "mitigated" or "limited" skepticism. As concerns the theoretical foundations of human knowledge, he accepts that the arguments of the skeptic are irrefutable, but he says that the mitigated skeptic will continue to hold the beliefs he must hold in order to live. So we must separate (1) rational evidence for our beliefs and (2) the psychology or origin of our beliefs. Our beliefs do not originate in reason or the intellect, says Hume, nor are they rationally justifiable. Our beliefs originate in human nature or natural instinctive forces, custom, habit, and education. Belief is more an act of the nonrational part of our nature than the rational. This is why skeptical arguments ultimately fail to undermine our beliefs: they are irrelevant, beside the point, for our beliefs are neither rational nor are they voluntarily held: we are forced by nature and custom to believe as we do.[8]

Some of Hume's claims about skepticism can be disputed, but some I find illuminating and helpful. For example, I accept his claims (1) that skepticism cannot be refuted on logical or philosophical grounds; (2) that it obviously cannot be taken seriously as an attitude that we should adopt and that it must therefore be refutable on some grounds; and (3) that the grounds on which it can be refuted are what I shall broadly call pragmatic grounds.

The easy of escaping the questions of the adequate skeptic is to ignore them altogether. But if this is done for no good reason, it is too simple an escape. It is capricious and philosophically indefensible. What must be done is to show by means of some good reason that there is a point where the infinite regress of questions must end. Again, I do not believe that logical reasons can be found that will accomplish this end, but perhaps pragmatic reasons can be suggested.

We need, at this point, a tentative definition of the term *faith*. Later I will attempt to provide a more precise definition of this term, but for present purposes let us simply say that *faith* is believing a proposition (1) that is not adequately supported by public evidence, and (2) for reasons other than the available public evidence. The reasons for the belief may be private pieces of evidence, pragmatic considerations, desires, or even prejudices.

Later in this study, having defined religious faith in terms of private evidence, I shall ask what legitimate role private evidence can play in evidence situations, if it can legitimately play any role. That is, I shall try to answer the question, Is it ever rational to base belief on private evidence? But a different point must be made first: I will now try to show that in the context of the searching questions skeptics can raise against some of the most commonly accepted conclusions of general knowledge, private evidence must be used if we are to "know" anything at all. That is, I will try to show that all knowledge is ultimately based on faith.

I will try to show that private evidence must be used in general knowledge as well as in religious faith, and that it therefore cannot be true that it is always irrational to have faith; unless (as some skeptics would argue) believing the conventionally accepted conclusions of general knowledge is irrational too. And the point will be that if it is not irrational to use private evidence as the ultimate ground for the acceptance of such a proposition as "The external world exists," then perhaps it is not irrational to use private evidence as the ultimate ground for such religious propositions as "A loving God exists." Of course, even if it is true that all knowledge is based on faith (private evidence) it will not immediately follow that religious faith is epistemologically justified. It may be that some kinds of faith (e.g., those upon which general knowledge is based) are rational and others (religious faith or faith simpliciter) irrational. I shall argue about this point later.

There are certain propositions that we normally do not bother to doubt and that we all agree can be "known."

(1) I know that this is a rose.
(2) I know the answer to that question.
(3) I know that Richard Nixon was President of the United States.
(4) I would know his face anywhere.
(5) I know what Jones would say to that.
(6) I know that apples are edible.

Of course there may be ways of doubting the truth of such propositions, that is, of doubting the things we obviously and paradigmatically "know." The adequate skeptic can raise troublesome questions about just such beliefs. But the point is that in the standard, optimum cases where everything seems in order and nothing seems awry, we have all agreed (all but the skeptic) that it is senseless to doubt the truth of such propositions.

As Cardinal Newman put it, "There are many truths in concrete matter which no one can demonstrate yet everyone unconditionally accepts."[9] In other words, there are beliefs we all hold, propositions we all claim to know, where we cannot substantiate our knowledge-claims. I would like to separate such beliefs into two categories: what I will call *ordinary beliefs* and *metaphysical beliefs*.

Let us take ordinary beliefs first. Here are some examples:

(7)   Moscow exists.
(8)   The earth is a revolving globe.
(9)   Apart from food I will die.
(10) Napoleon was defeated at Waterloo.
(11) Fire burns.

There are, of course, a good many ordinary beliefs for which a great deal of supporting evidence can be adduced. But the problem is that the evidence is never quite sufficient to answer all the questions of the adequate skeptic. Take proposition (10). All of us who are nonskeptics, I assume, are quite prepared to admit that we are justified in believing that Napoleon was defeated at Waterloo. Yet we would find ourselves in some difficulty if we were to try to convince someone that Napoleon was defeated at Waterloo who was not willing to accept the statements made in history textbooks. Of course there is good inductive evidence that most statements in history texts are reliable (so nonskeptics would claim), and so we have good reasons for accepting (10). But we would not be able to convince the adequate skeptic of this; he could keep challenging every bit of evidence we could elicit in support of our belief, and if the attainment of "knowledge" rests upon our ability to answer all the skeptic's questions, that is, if we must substantiate our knowledge-claim, we would never attain it.

Newman also said "Life is for action. If we insist on proofs for everything, we shall never come to action: to act you must assume, and that assumption is faith."[10] That is, we cannot be consistent skeptics and still live, and this is why there are ordinary beliefs which, though they can be doubted, we do not in normal cases bother to doubt them. There may be no conclusive and final epistemological grounds for our beliefs, but if we want to live we must hold them; if we did not our only recourse would be to lie down and die. Thus Hume says, "If we believe, that fire warms, or water refreshes, 'tis only because it costs us too much pain to think otherwise."[11] This of course does not show that our ordinary beliefs are all true beliefs; it shows only that we are in some sense justified in holding them, for we could not live unless we did.

Besides ordinary beliefs, there are also *metaphysical beliefs*. These are beliefs that carry great weight in formulating our interpretation of and attitude toward our experience. A *metaphysical belief* is like a pair of eyeglasses through which we "see" the world. A change in a person's metaphysical beliefs would involve a change in his conceptual framework. He would "see" the world differently. Let me list a few propositions that I take to be metaphysical beliefs for most of us:

(12)   Things retain their continuity in time.
(13)   Phenomena will behave tomorrow as they did yesterday.
(14)   Some of my experience is nonillusory.
(15)   Some of my memories are reliable.
(16)   The external world exists.
(17)   Other minds exist.
(18)   Propositions that seem self-evident to me are self-evident.

The fact that each of these propositions has attracted no little attention in the history of philosophy should be a clue to us that anyone who tried to prove one of them would face extreme difficulty. The skeptic can make us uncomfortable by raising questions about these assumptions that we cannot answer, not to mention that actual arguments can be raised against them. So we do not hold these and other metaphysical beliefs because they have been conclusively verified; we hold them because we need to in order to "see" the world fruitfully.

So metaphysical beliefs are unlike ordinary beliefs in that they are constitutive of our entire way of seeing the world (rather than simply instances of what we see in the world). But they are like many of our ordinary beliefs in that we cannot conclusively verify them when confronted with skeptical challenges.

How is it, then, that we justify our acceptance of beliefs that cannot be successfully defended against the skeptic? I have already suggested a partial answer to this question in terms of our "need" to accept them (pragmatic considerations), but I now propose to show that we also make use of private evidence in the process of becoming convinced of their truth.

When someone claims to know a proposition p, the strategy of the adequate skeptic—as we have seen—is to ask, "But how do you know p?" When the nonskeptic replies, "The ground for my acceptance of p is q," the skeptic asks, "Yes, but what is your ground for q?" In this way the skeptic forces the nonskeptic into an infinite regress, into giving reasons for his reasons, ad infinitum. And the moral is that since a knowledge-claim can be supported only by an infinitely long chain of arguments, no one can ever substantiate a knowledge-claim.

I believe that the adequate skeptic is completely victorious here. I see no way that his challenge ran be met on his own terms. I see no philosophical ground for successfully terminating the infinite regress he gets us into. This is why I claimed earlier that there are propositions that we simply do not bother to doubt, *though they can be doubted*. In other words, I am saying that what we conventionally do in response to skeptical challenges is resort to what may be called faith: we make certain knowledge-claims without bothering to substantiate them. Of course I am *not* saying that the adequate skeptic's strategy of "How do you know p?" is successful in that it gives us good reasons to doubt p, that is, in that it provides us with evidence *against* p. In a sense, the adequate skeptic remains entirely aloof from any attempt to refute knowldge-claims by producing evidence against them. So what I am claiming is not that the skeptic has given the nonskeptic good reasons to deny p; I am claiming that he has succeeded in asking questions (1) that the nonskeptic *must answer* if he is to vindicate his claim to know p, but (2) that he cannot answer apart from infinite regress. And it is in response to this predicament that I claim we conventionally resort to what amounts to faith.

Similarly, Ferre says:[12]

> If a skeptic insists on more and more grounds, rejecting as inadequate all that are offered . . . there comes a point at which the serious disputant must say: "The grounds I have given you are, it seems to me, sufficient to support my belief. I may be mistaken, but . . . now I must go about my business." *Where* this point is reached is, I think, theoretically indeterminate. There is an essential openendedness about the process of inquiry that foils every well-meaning attempt to draw neat lines of this sort. But precisely because lines cannot be drawn here, it may always seem to some that the arguments should have continued; they may feel that the illegitimate move, "I just know," has been used. This, however, is not the case. The primacy of the life-oriented domain over the theoretical simply means that somewhere we must say, "Here I stand, God helping me I can do no other," and then act on our beliefs in the full realization that they are *perhaps* actually false.

In other words, there comes a point in any argument with the adequate skeptic where the only move left for the nonskeptic is to say, "Since I am convinced of what I am saying and you are not, this is where sensible debate ends." This move is arbitrary in that the adequate skeptic's challenge has not been answered, but it is pragmatic in that life would cease if the argument were to continue infinitely. And this, I take it, is an appeal to private evidence, that is, to evidence that convinces the nonskeptic but not the adequate skeptic: "The evidence I have given thus far may seem inadequate to you but it utterly convinces me." It is private because it would not convince the consensus of rational persons, that is, persons acting on nothing but Russell's Principle, for Russell's Principle does not allow the wholehearted acceptance of a proposition p before the knowledge-claim "I know p" has been substantiated.

For example, probably the most common move is to cite that type of private evidence that might be called *evidence of testimony*. That is, we give evidence for p by citing an authority who (1) also affirms p, and (2) is presumably in a position to know whether or not p is true. This move is designed to stop the infinite regress the adequate skeptic gets us into, but the problem is that the evidence of testimony is private in that it is convincing only to those who accept (2). And of course the adequate skeptic can raise embarrassing questions about (2).

But in claiming that we resort to private evidence, that is, faith, I am not saying that we "close our minds." Since even in the context of our argument with the adequate skeptic we are under the authority of Russell's Principle, we must (if we want to be rational) welcome further evidence that might later be discovered that will bear on the truth of p. So we do not exactly say to the adequate skeptic, "I am convinced of the truth of p and you are not, and that is all there is to it." Rather, we say (or should say), "Since I am convinced of p, I am going to continue to affirm p *until you give me good reasons* to deny p, that is, until you come up with actual evidence against p."

In this light, it will be helpful to refer to a passage from C. S. Peirce's essay "The Fixation of Belief":[13]

That the settlement of opinion is the sole end of inquiry is a very important proposition. It sweeps away, at once, various vague and erroneous conceptions of proof. A few of these may be noticed here.
1. Some philosophers have imagined that to start an inquiry it was only necessary to utter a question. . . , and have even recommended us to begin studies with questioning everything! But the mere putting of a proposition

into the interrogative form does not stimulate the mind to any struggle after belief. There must be a real living doubt, and without this all discussion is idle.

2.   It is a very common idea that a demonstration must rest on some ultimately and absolutely indubitable propositions. . . . But in point of fact, an inquiry, to have that completely satisfactory result called demonstration, has only to start with propositions perfectly free from all actual doubt. If the premises are not in fact doubted at all, they cannot be more satisfactory than they are.

3.   Some people seem to love to argue a point after all the world is fully convinced of it. But no further advance can be made. When doubt ceases, mental action on the subject comes to an end; and, if it did go on, it would be without purpose.

As Fogelin points out,[14] Peirce is not claiming here that a proposition is true if no one doubts it, nor is he saying that knowledge rests on a set of propositions that in fact no one doubts. Indeed, Peirce's point can be made in the context of an admission that the adequate skeptic has achieved his goal of showing that no knowledge-claim can ever be completely vindicated. For what Peirce is saying is that just because we can call into question any proposition in the language by asking "How do you know it?" is no reason to doubt it. Thus Fogelin says:[15]

The person who claims to know something does commit himself to producing adequate reasons upon demand, but he does not commit himself to responding to pyrrhonistic scepticism by answering every question that can be generated by converting his reasons into questions. He claims to have reasons that no one will question, but not reasons that no one will ever question, or reasons that cannot be questioned because they are philosophically impeccable. In sum, it would be a mistake to try to avoid the theoretical possibility of an infinite regress of reasons within the very analysis of epistemic statements, for in the first place this will beg the question against fallibilism, and in the second place it ignores the fact that such statements are used in context where it is taken for granted that at least some things are known. The sceptic may still insist that we have no right to make the assumption that other things are known, and if he likes he may therefore declare all epistemic statements unfounded. The first part of philosophical wisdom is to recognize that without recourse to pragmatic considerations there is no way of answering the sceptic's challenge.

What I am claiming, then, is that the only legitimate response to the adequate skeptic's strategy is to appeal to these *pragmatic considerations;* the argument must stop somewhere, so why not stop it at the point where the skeptic ceases to give actual grounds for doubting our knowledge-claim and simply begins to ask of every successive piece of evidence we cite, "But how do you know it?" (For the adequate skeptic, who only asks questions and who never raises objections or contrary evidence, this point comes at the outset of the debate. Thus debate with him should never be allowed to commence in the first place.) And this, I believe, is a tacit appeal to private evidence, for when unpacked, the non-skeptic's argument runs, "Since I am utterly convinced of p and you are not, this is where fruitful debate must cease, for life must continue." That is, the nonskeptic is forced to resort to evidence for p that is convincing to him but is not convincing to all rational persons (certainly not to the skeptic) ; and this brings his cognitive attitude within our definition of faith.

We must affirm, then, either (1) that nothing at all can be known because no knowledge-claim can be substantiated or (2) that some things can be known but that knowledge is based on faith, that is, on halting the adequate skeptic's infinite regress of questions by appealing either to private evidence or to some pragmatic need to believe p. Does this mean that there is no such thing as knowledge, that our beliefs are never warranted? Again, if "I know p" means "I can substantiate my knowledge-claim by answering all the questions of the adequate skeptic," then knowledge cannot be had. But if "I know p" means something less than this (as I believe it does), we can have knowledge.

I would argue that we know a true belief p (1) when there is a maximum limit of evidence in favor of p beyond which searching for additional evidence would be pointless, and (2) when the limit has been reached, that is, when the available evidence for p is as good or convincing as it can or need be. If there is no such limit, that is, if I can always go on accumulating more and more evidence for p, always increasing the probability of p but never reaching grounds for certainty, or if there is such a maximum limit but it has not yet been reached, then belief in p is not knowledge that p.

The adequate skeptic can accept this scheme: he will simply argue (based on the nonskeptic's own notion that knowledge must be based upon adequate evidence) that there is no maximum limit of evidence for any nonevident proposition. All knowledge-claims, to be acceptable, must be substantiated, and to substantiate a claim to know p, the evidence for p must be substantiated, and the evidence for the evidence must be substantiated, et cetera. To counter this, nonskeptics typically accept conventional standards of limits of evidence; they simply legislate that at certain points (and there are loose and flexible but generally understood criteria where these points are reached) sensible debate ends, for life must continue. Life must be lived, and so a line is drawn: beyond this point (it is said), to continue the debate is madness. The skeptic can still ask his troublesome questions, but so what? I may still be in error, but I can legitimately affirm p, and my belief in p is knowledge that p, if I have made every reasonable (not every logically possible) test of p.

Sometimes the debate-stopping point is reached when an accepted ordinary belief is reached ("Fire warms") and sometimes when an accepted metaphysical belief is reached ("Unless there is good reason to think otherwise, my sense-perceptions are reliable"). This is an appeal to faith: to acceptance of an unproved belief. The skeptic will obviously doubt the belief, or at least will want to raise his usual questions about it, and Russell's Principle will not allow us to accept it in the absence of adequate supporting evidence. The nonskeptic will perhaps want to argue that we *have* adequate evidence for the belief. The skeptic can of course question this, but at an even deeper level he can point out that the agreed-upon standard of adequacy is accepted without adequate evidence; *its* acceptance is based on faith.

Thus "all knowledge is based on faith." It appears that we can view *knowledge* as belief based on beliefs that are accepted by all but philosophical skeptics; and we can view *faith* as belief based on beliefs that are not acceptable to the consensus of rational nonskeptics. (There are far more religious skeptics than philosophical skeptics.) Well then (we will want to ask at this point) , Can I or can I not know that, say, what I am now holding in my hand is a pencil? This proposition can be known provided that I accept certain other beliefs, for example, that my sense-perceptions are normally reliable. But the skeptic will not accept this belief; he will not agree that *it* is evident, and this is where faith comes in. The public evidence in support of the proposition "Davis is now holding a pencil in his hand" should convince anyone of its truth who accepts the relevant beliefs (and all nonskeptics normally do accept them) . But this evidence will not and should not convince the person who does not accept the relevant beliefs, namely, the adequate skeptic.

Kant once said:[16]

> It still remains a scandal to philosophy . . . that the existence of things outside of us . . . must be accepted merely on *faith,* and that, if anyone thinks good to doubt their existence, we are unable to counter his doubts by any satisfactory proof.

Kant is talking about particular sorts of knowledge-claim here, knowledge-claims about the reality of things external to our consciousness. But taking Kant's comment in a broader perspective, it can be seen from the argument of this chapter that I quite agree with Kant's analysis of the epistemic situation of the nonskeptic in relation to the adequate skeptic. Some kind of appeal to faith is necessary. The only reservation I have about Kant's remark is that I see nothing scandalous about the situation.

The obvious question that demands an answer at this point is, Precisely when is faith justified and when is it not? That is, when is it rational to have faith? We will take up this question presently. For now, all that we have determined is that such an appeal is justified for pragmatic reasons when it can be shown that there is a real need to believe p. If I must believe p, say, in order to live, then I am obviously justified in believing p.

NOTES

1. David Hume, *An Enquiry Concerning Human Understanding* (La Salle, Ill.: The Open Court Publishing Company, 1946), p. 7.

2. Ibid., pp. 30–39.

3. David Hume, *A Treatise of Human Nature* (Oxford: The Clarendon Press, 1965), pp. 183, 218, 268–69.

4. Ibid., pp. 181–83. Like Sextus, Hume is even willing to apply his skeptical conclusions to his own arguments. *Treatise*, p. 265.

5. Hume, *Enquiry*, p. 164.

6. Ibid., pp. 169–70; cf. *Treatise*, pp. 183, 187.

7. Hume, *Treatise*, p. 183. Hume also says of the skeptic that "it is certain that no man ever met with such an absurd creature." *Enquiry*, p. 158.

8. Hume, *Enquiry*, pp. 43–47. For a helpful discussion of Hume's skepticism and a comparison of Hume and Sextus, see Richard Popkin's "David Hume: His Pyrrhonism and His Critique of Pyrrhonism" in V. C. Chappell, ed., *Hume* (Garden City, N.Y.: Anchor Books, 1966), pp. 53–98.

9. John Henry Cardinal Newman, *An Essay in Aid of a Grammar of Assent* (Garden City, N.Y.: Image Books, 1955) , p. 136. Cf. pp. 148–50.

10. Ibid., p. 91.

11. Hume, *Treatise,* p. 270; cf. pp. 183, 218; *Enquiry,* pp. 158–76.

12. K. Bendall and F. Ferre, *Exploring the Logic of Faith* (New York: Association Press, 1962) , pp. 141–42.

13. *Charles S. Peirce: Selected Writings,* ed. Philip P. Wiener (New York: Dover Publications, Inc., 1958) , pp. 100–101.

14. Fogelin, *Evidence and Meaning,* p. 68.

15. Ibid., p. 69.

16. Immanuel Kant, *Critique of Pure Reason,* trans. Norman Kemp Smith (New York: St. Martin's Press, 1965) , p. 34.

4

The Nature of Religious Faith

How is faith related to evidence? That is, in the experience of the religious believer, how does faith originate and operate in terms of evidence? And how is faith related to knowledge? These are the questions to which I now wish to address myself.

As I mentioned in the Introduction, most epistemologists of religion approach these questions by asking about the relation of faith to *reason*. However, a look at the history of Christian philosophy reveals several thinkers who propose, either explicitly or implicitly, clearly delineated theories of faith and *evidence*.

Søren Kierkegaard (1813–1855), for example, seems to suggest that faith is *contrary* or *opposed to evidence*. He defines faith as "the objective uncertainty due to the repulsion of the absurd held fast in the passion of inwardness."[1] Evidence, for Kierkegaard, is destructive of faith, and for two reasons. In the first place, the kind of cognitive state involved in proving or giving evidence for propositions is what he calls "objective knowledge." Here the knower remains disinterested and detached from that which he knows. But religious truth must be known "subjectively," that is, with passion and commitment. So faith must be a free act of will, a "leap" that carries the thinker across the gap caused by lack of adequate evidence. Faith is a risk; to take away the risk by adducing proofs and evidence (as the rational apologist does) is an act of unfaith; it is to make faith into dispassionate knowledge.

And in the second place, Kierkegaard is convinced that the content of Christian faith is what he calls "the absolute paradox," that is, the doctrine that "God became man." Virtually a contradiction, this proposition cannot be proved and so can be held only by faith. Thus Kierkegaard ridicules all attempts to render evident the propositions that Christians believe. If a believer attempts to prove the existence of God, for example, Kierkegaard suggests that he would be much more honest if he were to admit the real reason that he believes in God: "Well, I know nothing more about it except that my father told me it was so."[2] The more proof, the less faith; the more certainty, the less passion, Kierkegaard seems to be saying. Evidence and faith are mutually exclusive.

Easily contrasted with this is the view of Thomas Aquinas (1225–1274), who holds that faith is *partially* (but not wholly) *based upon evidence*. In order to know God, Aquinas says, we must assent to certain propositions. Some of these propositions (e.g., "God exists") can be proved by human reason alone. But certain others (e.g., "God is three in one") can be known only because God has revealed them. Human reason can thus carry us part of the way to God, but faith—which is assent to the truths of revelation not because of evidence for them but because of the authority of God who reveals them—is necessary to complete the journey.

Faith, to Aquinas, is a mean between science (or direct "seeing") and opinion. That is, it is partly rational and partly volitional: its propositions are sufficiently evidenced to be rationally warranted but are sufficiently unevidenced still to require a decision of the will.[3] Faith cannot be caused by rational evidence (this would make it science), but the evidence in its favor can remove intellectual obstacles to faith (if not, faith would be mere opinion). So, unlike Kierkegaard, Aquinas held that Christian apologetics is a worthwhile enterprise—both the positive task of giving evidence in favor of Christian propositions and the negative task of defending them against criticism.

A view even more strongly contrastable with that of Kierkegaard is the theory of faith and evidence of John Locke (1632–1714). Locke seems to suggest that faith is *wholly based upon evidence*. He defines the terms *reason* and *faith* virtually as does Aquinas, and he also agrees that certain truths about religion can be proved by reason and that certain others, which cannot, must be revealed by God. If a proposition is revealed by God, it must be accepted, Locke says. But the problem is to distinguish those propositions which are actually revealed from those which merely purport to be revealed. And here, Locke insists, reason rules. He says,[4]

> Whatever God hath revealed is certainly true: no doubt can be made of it. This is the proper object of faith: but whether it be a *divine* revelation or no, reason must judge . . . . *Nothing that is contrary to, and inconsistent with, the clear and self-evident dictates of reason, has a right to be urged or assented to as a matter of faith.*

Simply believing or having an inner feeling that a proposition is from God does not make it so. What we must do is test any purported revealed truth; if evidence supports the claim, it should be accepted; if not, it should be rejected. Thus faith must always be regulated by evidence; indeed, Locke calls faith "assent founded upon the highest reason."[5]

Finally, mention might also be made of the contemporary English philosopher of religion John Hick. Hick believes that all apprehension of the external world is through what he calls acts of interpretation, acts through which we view something in a certain way, "see it as" something. Both knowledge and faith have this character: both are acts of interpretation through which a person apprehends the order, form, or meaning of his experience. Some kinds of interpretation are virtually given or necessary, for example, when I accept the reality of the external world. Through perception, the external world in a sense forces itself upon me: I cannot avoid interpreting my experience as containing people, trees, and other such objects. But religious interpretation—the act of interpreting one's experience as experience of God—is totally voluntary. In no sense are we coerced into interpreting our experience in this way. Faith does not discover new facts about the world: it simply orders and interprets the facts in a religious way. In fact, the believer and the nonbeliever *agree* about all the facts they experience in the world: their differences are over the proper interpretation of the facts.

The evidence for and against the religious interpretation of life, Hick says, seems to be evenly balanced. The evidence that we encounter is ambiguous, "constituting permissive evidence both for theism and for naturalism."[6] Every experience of life can be interpreted either religiously or irreligiously. The act of religious interpretation, therefore, is primarily unevidenced and unevidenceable. It may be based on "permissive evidence" (evidence that allows it), but not on "conclusive evidence" (evidence that proves it). Thus Hick, a Christian, is not averse to admitting that Christianity is no more intellectually respectable than such other world views as naturalism or Buddhism.

These, then, are outlines of some of the theories of faith and evidence that we find among Christian philosophers. It is now time that I developed my own view—a theory that will be influenced in part by each of the above philosophers. For example, from Kierkegaard I accept the claim that a person is much more likely to have religious faith on the basis of what I call private evidence (e.g., his parents' word) than on the basis of public evidence. With Kierkegaard and Hick I am willing to admit that, on the basis of rational public evidence, Christianity cannot be shown to be more philosophically acceptable than other world views. And this agrees with Aquinas's admission that some of the truths of Christian faith cannot be proved. I accept Hick's claims that religious knowing differs only in content from other kinds of knowing, and that, since proof is lacking, every experience of life can be interpreted either religiously or irreligiously. And, finally, I agree with Locke that faith is warranted only if it is supported by the available evidence—though of course my willingness to include private evidence in the scheme modifies what Locke would have meant by the phrase *supported by evidence.*

Let us define the term *conviction* as a deep-seated acceptance of the truth of a given proposition, a tenaciously held belief. That is, to hold a conviction is to be firmly persuaded of the truth of a proposition; it is to accept the proposition as indubitably true. By the phrase *deep-seated acceptance,* I mean simply that a conviction is a belief held so firmly that a change in one's convictions does not occur easily, and in a sense is a real change in oneself. For example, I take it that the following kinds of propositions are often held as convictions:

(1) Ireland is a fine country.
(2) Every event has a cause.
(3) Murder is wrong.
(4) The American way is best.
(5) My mother loves me.
(6) My friends will not let me down.
(7) Picasso was a great artist.
(8) Hitler was used by the Devil.
(9) A loving God exists.

These kinds of propositions are convictions if they are so firmly imbedded in the belief-structure of a given individual that he will not easily give them up, and can not give them up without becoming virtually a changed person.

The term *conviction* has been the subject of some discussion in recent years, especially in theological circles. I want to avoid an error that has been made by some theologians in their attempts to defend religious language against the criticisms of certain philosophers. The error is that of somehow supposing that to speak of religious language as "convictional" is to free us from concerns about the truth and falsity of religious propositions. For surely convictions must be "of" or "in" something: otherwise it is difficult to understand what convictions are. And surely what a given conviction is in can be expressed in terms of propositions that the holder of the conviction will hold as true precisely because they express his conviction. Thus to speak of the convictional functions of religious language is not to escape issues of truth or falsity, as some theologians may have supposed.

The term *faith* is used in a great variety of ways in ordinary language. For example, sometimes it is used to refer to a given system of beliefs or religion: "He holds to the Islamic faith." At other times the term seems to contain moral connotations, as in "One should always act in good faith" or "Failure to appear would be a breach of faith." And very commonly, the term seems to refer to an attitude of trust or confidence—say, in a given person. This usage (which, in theological contexts, is identical with *fiducia*) is almost always "faith in" or (synonymously) "belief in," as, for example, "He has faith in the common voter," "I can help you if only you believe in me."

But another usage is equally common and is more directly relevant to our concerns in this essay: that usage which seems to refer to an actual cognitive state, a conviction or belief or opinion (in theological contexts, *fides*). This usage is almost always "faith *that*" or (again synonymously) "belief *that*." It is interesting to note that faith statements of this sort (we might call them *cognitive* uses of *faith*) seem to vary greatly in the degree to which they are supported by evidence. Sometimes such statements seem to be clearly contrary to evidence or at least only weakly supported by evidence.

(a) I still can't bring myself to believe my brother is dead.
(b) Every season, Jones has faith that the Padres will win the pennant.

Sometimes they seem to be not susceptible to proof and seem to be such that evidence is largely irrelevant to them.

    (c)   All we can do is accept on faith that father will not be killed in the war.

    (d)   I don't know that I'm going to pass the exam, but I have faith that I will.

And at other times they seem to be clearly based upon evidence or are at least clearly assumed to be based upon evidence.

    (e)   Bobby Fisher has a great deal of faith in his end game.

    (f)   I believe it is beginning to rain.

But despite this wide variety of evidence-situations in which *faith* and *belief* can be employed in their cognitive usage (faith that p is true), it is clear that their main use is in evidence-situations of the types 2, 3, 4, or 5 described in chapter 1. There are uses where it could be argued that the evidence-situation is of type 1 (e), but perhaps these are as much *trust* as *cognitive* uses. Where the use is clearly cognitive, "faith that p" is mainly used in situations where the evidence is either ambiguous on the truth of p or else clearly supports not-p. Where there is adequate or nearly adequate public evidence in support of p, some other term than *faith* (e.g., *knowledge*) will normally be used to indicate the cognitive state involved in affirming p.

But another point should be made as well. Despite the wide variety of evidence-situations in which the terms *faith* and *belief* are used in their cognitive senses, I think there is a common thread running through them all: *at no time does a person have faith that p when he is not satisfied that acceptance of p is warranted.* That is, faith can and does begin only when a person is satisfied that he ought to have faith. Apart from the conviction that it is (so far as he can see) justified and warranted, faith cannot arise. No person can or will have faith that p as long as he thinks that acceptance of p would be irrational or silly. And the most obvious criterion by which a person can decide whether faith that p is warranted or not is of course the evidence he encounters for and against p. Faith can originate only when a person encounters what seems to him adequate evidence to warrant it.

I therefore propose to define faith in terms of private evidence. With some cognitive faith statements the relevant evidence seems public in nature, as in (e), but as I mentioned, perhaps (e) is really an example of the *trust* usage. If so, it would then appear that *cognitive* uses of *faith* are virtually always (and not just usually) based on private evidence. And as I shall argue presently, this is what distinguishes faith from knowledge. Furthermore, faith is conviction based on what is seen to be (by the possessor of faith) adequate evidence to warrant it. People have faith when they are satisfied that they ought to have faith. Thus faith is *conviction based on adequate private evidence.*

This runs directly contrary to the claims of Kierkegaard, who seemed at times to suggest that Christians hold to their beliefs despite conclusive evidence against their beliefs *of which they are fully aware.* But it does not seem to me that this is so: I for one am quite sure that if I became aware of evidence that convinced me that my religious beliefs were false I would give them up. Faith does not seem to me blind and unreasoning, as Kierkegaard implies. In fact, I find it difficult to believe that it is even *possible* for a person to believe p while convinced that belief in p is unwarranted. I do not wish to insist dogmatically on this point: perhaps in some sense it is possible. I simply do not see how. Religious believers (along with everybody else), I think, believe as they do because they are convinced by public and/or private evidence that their beliefs are warranted.

But in claiming that faith is based upon what the believer sees as "adequate evidence" I am not setting up an objective standard of adequacy, nor am I saying that when the evidence for a faith-proposition reaches such a level, people will invariably believe. No; the point is rather that a person believes when he encounters what is *for him* adequate evidence. If the term *adequate* is too ambiguous, the term *convincing* will do. Faith is based on what is, for the possessor of faith, *convincing* evidence. And, as we saw in chapter 1, convincing evidence can be as much private as public. Some people require more evidence than others, but anyone who has faith does so because the evidence he has encountered—public or private—has satisfied him that faith is warranted. No conviction is possible without convincing evidence.

So the concept of *adequate evidence* should not be confused with *proof*. The evidences encountered in *any* evidence-situation are rarely logically compelling; often, they are not even public. It is not the degree or amount of evidence that is important (thus far in this essay), but the fact that it is convincing to an individual. It may be true that no person can prove that what he believes is true, but still a person believes because the evidence has convinced him that he ought to believe. For example, take the case of a nonbeliever in religion who, let us say, hears a sermon and then decides to believe. Why does he believe, whereas before he did not? I am claiming that it is because the available evidence (public or private) satisfies him that what the preacher says is true. If he knows that the preacher is a fool or a liar, or if he has other grounds for doubting what the preacher says, he will not believe. Or, take the case of a believer in religion who was raised in a religious home. Why does he believe in God? Perhaps, as Kierkegaard suggests, it is because his parents, whom he loved and trusted, told him about God. If the child felt that the parents were untrustworthy, he may well have rejected their testimony. The child believes because evidence tells him that his parents' word is trustworthy, and because he has never encountered sufficient contrary evidence to warrant disbelief.

Many have suggested that faith is accepting a proposition as true on insufficient evidence. I do not find this embarrassing; indeed if public evidence is meant, the suggestion is quite true. But if insufficient *private* evidence is meant, or evidence *seen as insufficient by the believer,* it is not faith at all. If such a cognitive act is possible (which I doubt), perhaps we should call it gullibility. As Charles Craig says:[7]

> We must not confuse faith with credulity. You cannot believe what you know is not true. It can of course be alleged that Christian faith . . . rests on inadequate grounds, or that the evidence in behalf of one's faith is inadequate. It is one thing to say that, but it is quite another to say that a person's faith is based on inadequate grounds of which he himself is aware. To believe, to have faith, on grounds the inadequacy of which we are conscious, is really an impossibility. If evidence appears to us as adequate, we are convinced, and vice versa. If we are not convinced, faith or belief does not exist for us.

It is true that one person will believe on grounds deemed inadequate by another. But anyone who believes on grounds he sees as inadequate (if this is possible) is not practicing faith. An old joke mentions the child who defined faith as "believing what you know ain't true." But I deny that this is faith, for someone who assents to a proposition he knows is not true (if this is possible) is not basing belief on what he sees to be adequate evidence.

Again I must point out that I am not here speaking of objective standards of rationality. In saying that faith is based on what is seen by the believer to be adequate evidence, I am not denying that faith can be irrational or unfounded. These matters will be taken up later in this study. And in my expressions of doubt that in any clear sense a person can ever believe "what he knows ain't true," I am not denying that people ever are "gullible." Here, however, *gullibility* has a different meaning. It is obvious that people can be and often are "gullible" in the sense that they fail to follow Russell's Principle; that is, they assent to propositions that are not supported by the available evidence. But I strongly doubt that in any clear sense people ever disobey the amended version of Russell's Principle stated in chapter 1:

Give to any hypothesis that is worth your while to consider just that degree of credence which the evidence *as you see it* warrants.

It will be recalled that in chapter 2 we investigated the notion of knowledge and saw that there are usually said to be three criteria that must be satisfied before a cognitive state reaches the level of knowledge. Roughly, so it is claimed, I know p if and only if (1) I believe p; (2) p is true; and (3) I have adequate evidence for p. Let us ignore the difficulties that philosophers have encountered in trying to come up with precise criteria of knowledge. One clear moral nevertheless to be drawn from our investigation is that there are no set rules for what constitutes adequate evidence; it depends upon the proposition in question, for different types and degrees of evidence are required in different contexts. But *knowledge* is never based on inadequate evidence: a cognitive state reaches the level of knowledge only when the evidence is as good as it can or need be, when further investigation is pointless.

How then does knowledge differ from faith, that is, what is the relationship between knowledge and "conviction based on adequate private evidence"? In answering this question, I think the simplest procedure will be to take each of the three claimed criteria of knowledge and see to what extent faith does or does not meet the requirement. Let us take the second criterion first, since only a brief comment is needed. It is obvious that while no false proposition can be "known," a person can believe or have faith in a false proposition. Thus faith does not meet the requirement of the second criterion of knowledge. "Jones knows p, but not-p" is contradictory, but "Jones believes p, but not-p" and "Jones has faith that p, but not-p" are not.

The third criterion, that of adequate evidence, also affords a clear way of distinguishing faith from knowledge. As we saw above, faith-propositions are typically based on *private* evidence. But of course *knowledge* must be based on *public* evidence: that is, a proposition can be known to be true only if it is based not upon what the knower subjectively sees as adequate evidence (which leaves room for privacy) but upon what is conventionally agreed by the users of ordinary language to constitute adequate evidence. But Bendall makes an important point in this regard:[8]

> There is a sense, I would hold, in which what may count as evidence in critical inquiry must be *public,* but even this can be interpreted too restrictively. Suppose, for example, that an astronomer reports observing by the naked eye twelve meteorites in a certain region of the sky during a certain period, but that no one else happens to have been looking then and there to check his report. This observation is in a certain sense "private" and unrepeatable; nevertheless his report *may* be regarded as a reliable datum for astronomy. This is because his observation is in another sense "public"—namely, in that there are well-established procedures which *anyone* could employ for checking such a report. Trial lawyers and psychologists are the recognized specialists in the most obvious procedures applicable in this case, but such procedures are in principle applicable by anyone. . . . The important requirement is only that what is counted as evidence be itself tied down at various points to a broader ground of experience, and accredited by critical examination by an indefinitely wide community of inquirers.

This agrees with the traditional view in the philosophy of science that scientific propositions must be based on the evidence of observation (either directly or indirectly) to be accepted. That is, a proposition must be either directly based on observation or else it must entail consequences supported by observed states-of-affairs.

The first criterion, that of belief, raises certain difficulties. Let me introduce here a distinction between *certainty* and *certitude.* I shall define certitude as the state of being utterly convinced of the truth of a given proposition and *certainty* as the state of being utterly convinced of the truth of a given proposition *and* the state of being correct in one's conviction that the proposition is true; which means that *certainty* coincides with *knowledge* to the extent that the true belief is based on adequate evidence. These of course are technical definitions; I do not claim that they reflect ordinary usage.

The claim has often been made that knowledge gives one a higher degree of certainty than faith. This is perhaps an inaccurate way of expressing the point; perhaps "When one knows, one is certain; but when one has faith, one is not necessarily certain" would be a better way of expressing it. But at any rate, I agree with the point. Indeed, it follows from my definitions of *faith* and *knowledge*. And the further claim has also been made that faith often gives one as much certitude as does knowledge, and that this makes faith irrational, since we do not know with faith (as we do with knowledge) that the certitude is warranted. There are several complicated issues entangled here, and I do not propose to deal with them in detail. I simply wish to point out that faith and knowledge both involve psychological certitude, for both cognitive states base belief on what appears to the subject to be adequate evidence (though with faith the subject may be wrong that the evidence is adequate while with knowledge the subject cannot be wrong; otherwise he is not knowing). What my view of faith and evidence does, then, is show how people can have certitude in faith without having conclusive public evidence verifying their beliefs. They possess *certitude,* I claim, because a set of private evidences that they deem adequate convinces them that their beliefs are warranted. Thus if the first criterion of knowledge, that of belief, entails only what I have called *certitude,* faith does fulfill the requirement. For it is obvious that people are often utterly convinced that their faith-propositions are true. But if the belief criterion refers also to what I have called *certainty,* faith does not fulfill the requirement. For it is also obvious that people often place their faith in propositions that turn out to be false.

Faith, then, begins with what the believer sees as adequate evidence. However, it does seem to be characteristic of propositions that are accepted on faith that once they are accepted it is difficult for the believer later to be convinced that they should be rejected. They seem to become so firmly held as to be immune to falsification. This somehow seems characteristic of "faith-situations," that is, situations where a person accepts a proposition with complete certitude, despite the fact that the public evidence supporting the proposition is weak.

The difficulty this raises, however, is the problem of *bliks,* a term coined by R. M. Hare in the famous "theology and falsification" debate of the 1950s.[9] We have seen that supporting (public or private) evidences get faith going, but the problem is that, once a person has faith, contrary evidences will not usually force him to cease believing. That is, a person who believes because of certain convincing bits of evidence will not usually stop believing even if he is later confronted with powerful evidence counting against his beliefs. Once begun, faith often does take on the characteristics of a *blik,* an assumption or belief that cannot be refuted or falsified by contrary evidence—indeed, an assumption or belief to which public evidence no longer seems even relevant as regards verification or falsification.

I do not intend to deal here with the "theology and falsification" debate: I will take up this question in chapter 10, where I will qualify some of the admissions I am making here. What I would like to show, however, is simply that on two counts it would seem quite natural that even a faith "based on adequate private evidence" could (once begun) take on far more certainty than the public evidence strictly warrants. The first reason that the certitude of faith often transcends its evidential basis is that the content of faith-propositions is typically of very profound and intimate concern to the individual. The believer's *faith*—whether religious or secular— is very often part of his personal "reason for being," his own self-image. Little wonder, then, that our ultimate commitments can become *bliks.* The certitude of a Communist that Communism is the best economic system is often completely immune to contrary evidence, as is the certitude of an Irishman that Ireland is a fine country, or the certitude of a Christian that Christ rose from the dead and still lives today. Our personal commitments and deepest concerns, whether religious or secular, often become *bliks* because our own personal identities are involved in the *bliks*. We can no more easily give up such a *blik* than we can easily give up our own self-image.

The second reason that faith-propositions are often held with more certitude than the evidence strictly warrants is that the believer, in having faith, often experiences a total transformation of his way of seeing life. As Hick argues, faith is a "total interpretation"; the believer experiences all of his life as being lived in the presence of God.[10] The experience of finding God is for him like putting on a new set of glasses through which to "see" the world—it is like having an illusion (of God's absence) removed. Thus faith often does possess more certitude than is evidentially warranted: it opens up an entire new outlook on life that goes far beyond the original act of faith that was made possible by private evidence.

It is true, then, that the certitude people feel that their faith-propositions are true is often stronger than the public evidence strictly warrants. This characteristic of faith-propositions has led some philosophers to criticize them by denying their cognitive status. Again, I will deal with this criticism in chapter 10. The point I wish to make here, however, is that this characteristic is not peculiar to propositions made in the context of religion (as some critics have claimed). Such a criticism could be made of any proposition that either (1) was a "total" interpretation or (2) had been incorporated into the believer's personal self-understanding. Thus such a proposition as "All events are caused" can become a *blik* on the ground of (1) and such a proposition as "Ireland is a fine country" can become a *blik* on the ground of (2). And neither is a religious proposition on any standard interpretation of the term *religious*.

Hence the certitude of faith often does go beyond its evidential basis. But this is not to say that its content does;

that is, this does not imply that in faith people believe un-evidenced propositions. A person may be more sure of an article of faith than the evidence strictly entitles him to be, but he will not believe an article of faith that is not sup-ported by what he sees as convincing evidence.

Faith, then, is conviction based on convincing private evidence. Religious faith is conviction based on convincing private evidence on religious matters. If this is an accurate description of the epistemological nature of faith, we still have before us the question whether faith, thus defined, is ever epistemologically justified or rational. To that question we shall now turn.

NOTES

1. Soren Kierkegaard, *Concluding Unscientific Postscript* (Princeton, N.J.: Princeton University Press, 1941), p. 540.

2. Ibid., p. 491.

3. Thomas Aquinas, *On the Truth of the Catholic Faith (Summa Contra Gentiles)* (Garden City, N.Y.: Hanover House, 1955–1957), 3. 40. 4.

4. John Locke, *An Essay Concerning Human Understanding,* ed. Alex-ander Fraser, 2 vols. (Oxford: The Clarendon Press, 1894), bk. 4, chap. 18, §10. (italics Lockes's).

5. Ibid., bk. 4, chap. 16, p. 14.

6. John H. Hick, *Faith and Knowledge,* 2d ed. (Ithaca, N.Y.: Cornell University Press, 1966), p. 162.

7. Charles H. Craig, "A Layman's Definition of Faith," *The Review and Expositor* 49 (April 1952):154.

8. Bendall and Ferre, *Exploring the Logic of Faith,* p. 108.

9. See A. Flew and A. MacIntyre, *New Essays in Philosophical Theology* (New York: The Macmillan Company, 1964), pp. 96–103.

10. Hick, *Faith and Knowledge,* p. 146.

Part II
James and the Right to Believe

5

Intellectualism and "The Will to Believe"

We turn now to the problem of discovering whether or not faith is ever epistemologically justified. I shall argue that there are circumstances where it is fully rational to have faith, and my line of reasoning will be influenced by a noted argument of the American philosopher William James (1842–1910). This argument is found most centrally in his famous essay "The Will to Believe" (1897), and in others of his early essays, especially "The Sentiment of Rationality" (1879) and "Is Life Worth Living?" (1895).[1] My aim in Part II will be to analyze this argument in detail and defend it against criticisms. Then in Part III I propose to use aspects of an amended version of the argument to defend the rationality of religious faith.

I wish to emphasize the point that I will be concerned here almost exclusively with views James held *prior* to his explicit avowal of pragmatism. I mention this point for two reasons: (1) because the Jamesian arguments I will discuss do not presuppose the so-called pragmatic theory of truth that James later advocated, and (2) because in his pragmatic period James attempted to defend religious faith in quite a different way than he did in "The Will to Believe." There are some points of similarity, and it is probably true that the early essays helped James along the path that eventually led him to pragmatism. But I think that those interpreters are mistaken who read the early essays by the light of James's later pragmatism. The early essays can and should be allowed to stand on their own.

When James wrote "The Will to Believe," the essay stirred up an immediate controversy, and in the intervening years it has enjoyed a wide reading and has been reprinted many times. The controversy, of course, has now died down, but it does not seem to me that the issues James raised have been settled, and one still finds occasional articles or book chapters devoted to refuting or defending James.

I first read "The Will to Believe" as a senior in college. I remember having two distinct impressions from that initial reading. The first was that James had not succeeded in making a good case for his thesis. I felt that his intentions in the essay were not made so clear as they might have been, that some of his examples were more puzzling than helpful, and that several key ambiguities in his argument were entirely passed over, apparently without his having noticed them. But my second impression was that what James was *trying* to say in this essay was correct. I still feel essentially the same way.

James's essay has unfortunately succeeded in confusing many of its readers, and has been interpreted in an amazingly wide variety of ways, some of which I shall argue are hopelessly wrong. For example, some early critics claimed that the force of James's argument was to justify the worst kind of capricious, wishful thinking: "I have the right to believe whatever I want to believe because I will to believe it." James vigorously denied this charge and was convinced for the rest of his life that his essay was misinterpreted mainly because of its catchy but misleading title. Accordingly, he came to regret having chosen the title "The Will to Believe," wishing instead that he had chosen some such title as "The Duty to Believe" or "A Defense of Faith" or, best of all, "The Right to Believe."[2]

Perhaps there was some justification for James's regret about the title,[3] but the title is not by any means all that is at fault. The fact that James was misinterpreted is due more to the ambiguity of the essay itself than to its title. What I shall try to do in Part III, then, is (1) attempt to restate as precisely as possible what I take to be the essential logic of James's thesis, and (2) argue that this thesis is sound and acceptable.

In "The Will to Believe" James is interested in a particular kind of evidence-situation, namely, the type I called in chapter 1 case (3), that is, the situation where evidence is either absent altogether on the truth of a given proposition or else is present but ambiguous. He is particularly interested in religious propositions that fit case (3), though he does not limit himself to religious propositions, nor do his arguments apply only to them. The main thesis of his essay is that we are sometimes epistemologically justified in holding a belief on grounds other than the available evidence, where the truth or falsity of the belief has not been established by an appeal to the available evidence and cannot at present be established by such an appeal. Thus it can be seen that at heart "The Will to Believe" constitutes an attack on Russell's Principle: it is an attempt to show us that the Principle does not always hold, need not always guide us.

I take it that this is what James means when he tells us that he is arguing in opposition to views like that held by W. K. Clifford.[4] In what would clearly count as a version of Russell's Principle, Clifford declared: "It is wrong always, everywhere, and for anyone, to believe anything upon insufficient evidence."[5] Against this view, what James tries to do is defend the "right to believe" (or better, the rationality or epistemological justification of believing) a proposition that is not adequately supported by evidence.

It is now recognized that there are two distinct arguments or doctrines in "The Will to Believe." It is interesting, and perhaps instructive, that neither James nor his early interpreters noticed the distinction. The first philosopher to distinguish between the two doctrines was Gail Kennedy, whose paper "Pragmatism, Pragmaticism, and The Will To Believe —A Reconsideration,"[6] was first made public in 1956, some sixty years after "The Will to Believe" appeared. Following Kennedy's terminology, I shall distinguish between (1) the "will to believe": the doctrine that belief or faith is sometimes self-verifying, that is, the doctrine that a willingness to act as if p were true can at times either make p true or be a factor in making p true; and (2) the "right to believe": the doctrine that in certain circumstances we are epistemologically justified in believing more than the evidence strictly warrants.

I shall deal with both doctrines and shall ask how, if at all, the two are related in James's overall argument. But the second doctrine, I think, is more philosophically interesting, and is much more relevant to the argument I shall develop in Part III. Accordingly, most of Part II will be devoted to analyzing and evaluating the "right to believe" doctrine.

James acutely points out that there are two great epistemological rules that we must follow if we are to attain knowledge, and these rules constitute our two most basic duties in all cognitive matters. They are (1) believe truth, and (2) avoid error. Now it is clear that in most cases the two rules agree; that is, the behavior entailed by obeying the one would also be entailed by obeying the other. But the difficulty is that there are cases where the rules disagree, where obeying one would entail very different behavior from that entailed by obeying the other. In other words, there are cases where a person must decide which of the two rules he is going to obey.

Returning to my categorization of evidence-situations, it is clear that in case (1), for example, the two rules agree. In a case (1) kind of evidence situation, if a person adopted the cognitive attitude of affirming p he would simultaneously be satisfying both rules. But in case (3), and in the subcategories near case (3) (i.e., where there is, say, a very slight preponderance of evidence for p over not-p), a person would have to decide which rule he was going to obey. He could avoid error by deciding to affirm nothing at all—that is, neither p nor not-p—but in doing so he would also insure that he would not believe truth. This would be the proper attitude for the person who wants to avoid error more than he wants to believe truth. But for the person who wants to believe truth more than he wants to avoid error, running the risk of affirming p would be the proper attitude.

We might distinguish between two sorts of thinkers here, the *venturesome* thinker, who holds that the "believe truth" rule takes priority in situations of conflict between the two rules, and the *cautious* thinker, who holds that the "avoid error" rule takes priority in situations of conflict. The venturesome thinker is willing to run the risk of being in error on the chance of gaining knowledge. He will hold many beliefs: many of his beliefs will be correct, but he will occasionally be in error too. This philosophy is clearly acceptable: we want to believe true propositions. The cautious thinker plays it safe. He holds few beliefs—only those of which he is absolutely certain—and thus fails to believe many propositions. But his strong point is that he is seldom in error. This philosophy is acceptable too: we want to avoid error.

The important question, then, is: Which rule takes priority? Obviously there is no provable answer to this question, for these two rules are the most basic rules of all in epistemology. There are no other, more basic, rules than these by which we could test any possible answer. As Aristotle showed with the laws of logic, once we have arrived at the most basic axioms of all, the question of proof can no longer be raised.

But where the two rules conflict, we must make a decision on which one takes priority. Any such decision, James insists, is going to be a decision based not on reason (for there is no proof here), but on what he calls "the passional nature." What, then, is the "passional nature"? It is unfortunate that James never tells us, for he uses this term frequently in his argument. The term seems to have a rather broad meaning for James, including those human needs that might roughly be called emotional, moral, aesthetic, religious, or practical.

(James cites Pascal approvingly in "The Will to Believe," and perhaps the passional nature is close to what Pascal meant by "the heart.") Furthermore, the passional nature either includes or is very closely related to what James calls the "volitional nature," which means the facility of choice. It can be seen, then, that the passional nature for James includes a great deal (which is perhaps why it seems at times to be synonymous with "the whole man"), but what is clearly meant to be *excluded* is the intellect or "intellectual nature." In fact, the term *passional nature* seems to receive whatever meaning it has in James primarily by its opposition to the intellect or "pure intellect." For what James is leading to, as we shall soon see, is the claim that the passional nature is sometimes justified in determining belief. That is, what a person believes can at times be lawfully determined by his will on the basis of his needs or hopes. This is meant to be taken as contradicting those who claim that only the intellect can ever justifiably determine belief.

It is clear that many philosophers have decided that the "avoid error" rule takes priority over the "believe truth" rule—Clifford, for example. The most extreme case is of course Descartes, who decided to doubt everything that it is possible to doubt, that is, everything that is not absolutely indubitable and certain. Such a position is simply the strongest possible interpretation of Russell's Principle, together with the strongest possible insistence that the Principle always holds, which is what James is arguing against in "The Will to Believe."

James is conscious of the fact that such a philosophical point of view might take many forms. He refers to such positions by several different names: usually *intellectualism* or *skepticism*, sometimes *positivism* or *agnostic positivism*, or the *scientific attitude* or *rationalism*. He is convinced, however, that the epistemological basis of such views is essentially the same, and it is the burden of much of his work in philosophy, both early in his career and later, that such an epistemological basis is mistaken. For example, in an essay entitled "Faith and the Right to Believe," which was published as an appendix to *Some Problems of Philosophy*,[7] James characterizes Intellectualism as the acceptance of two postulates. The first is that the duty to avoid error always takes priority over the duty to believe truth. Thus faith, in the sense of risking belief in a hypothesis before the hypothesis is adequately evidenced, is excluded altogether. The rule is: Never believe anything on the basis of insufficient evidence; better to gain nothing by venturing nothing where there is a risk of error. The second postulate is that the universe is complete in itself prior to and apart from our apprehension of it. The world is "given," and it is our duty to apprehend what is given. In no sense does the character of the world depend on our cognitive attitude toward it. In order to gain knowledge, what is really needed, therefore, is a "passively receptive mind." Beliefs about the world are "mere externalities" that do not alter the significance of the rest of the world. This is why our personal preferences should play no part in our apprehension of the world.

James is willing to admit that there is much to be said for Intellectualism. In most evidence-situations, it is the attitude that is obviously called for. But the problem is that there are also evidence-situations where such an attitude is not called for. Intellectualism, says James, "is a safe enough position *in abstracto*. If a thinker had no stake in the unknown, no vital needs, to live or languish according to what the unseen world contained, a philosophic neutrality and refusal to believe either one way or the other would be his wisest cue. But, unfortunately, neutrality is not only inwardly difficult, it is also outwardly unrealizable, where our relations to an alternative are practical and vital."[8]

James has four arguments against Intellectualism, or against those who believe that Intellectualism is always the only proper attitude in evidence-situations. The first is that Intellectualism is itself established or accepted by the Intellectualist on passional rather than intellectual grounds. Choosing Intellectualism over its alternatives is not a matter of intellect over passion: it is simply a matter of choosing one passion over another. "The agnostic 'thou shalt not believe without coercive sensible evidence,' " James says, "is simply an expression (free to anyone to make) of private personal appetite for evidence of a peculiar kind."[9] Furthermore, the Intellectualist's claim that the universe is whole and complete apart from the knower, and that passion, as opposed to passive receptiveness, is a disturber of truth, "is itself an act of faith of the most arbitrary kind."[10] And since Intellectualism is the position that acts of faith are never epistemologically justified, it follows that Intellectualism is contradictory.

The second objection is closely related to the first: it is the undeniable fact that we do, in fact, use what might be called faith in gaining knowledge, where faith is again understood as the acceptance of a proposition not conclusively supported by evidence. In fact, James says, most of the everyday decisions of life are made on a nonintellectual basis. Our reasons for living, he says, are often "ludicrously incommensurate with the volume of our feeling, yet on the latter we unhesitatingly act."[11] The decision to believe a proposition, therefore, is not entirely a matter of the intellect—the "will," the "whole man", the "passional nature," the "personal temperament" of the subject come into play as well.[12] But it should also be noticed that faith, bias, passion not only come into play in the concerns of ordinary living: they are also involved in establishing some of the most basic assumptions of science, for example, the assumption of the uniformity of nature.[13] Intellectualism, then, is simply unrealistic when it attempts to legislate faith and passion out of evidence-situations.

James's third criticism of Intellectualism is that it is too rigid. Anyone who adopts it will find himself missing truths he might have gained had he been willing to run an epistemological risk or two. In fact, many of the most important truths in life are quite unprovable. Intellectual values are not the only values there are, and so the effect of Intellectualism is simply to guarantee that the Intellectualist will miss out on many of life's larger and richer opportunities. The Intellectualist rule "believe no unverified propositions," James admits, is normally a sound rule that maximizes right thinking and minimizes errors, but there are cases where following this rule will ensure failure to gain the truth. In certain of these cases (the limits of which we shall come to presently), James says, the rule is not a prudent rule: "A rule of thinking which would absolutely prevent me from acknowledging certain kinds of truth if those kinds of truth were really there, would be an irrational rule."[14]

Following the policy of running no risks would lead to our losing the truth of those propositions which are unverified but true. We might succeed in avoiding error in this way, but we would also miss out on many of life's important truths. In such cases, what we need, then, is a little courage. We need to act in terms of our hopes (of gaining certain truths) rather than in terms of our fears (of being in error). Thus James says, "Dupery for dupery, what proof is there that dupery through hope is so much worse than dupery through fear? I, for one, can see no proof; and I simply refuse obedience to the scientist's command to imitate his kind of option, in a case where my own stake is important enough to give me the right to choose my own form of risk."[15]

James's third objection to Intellectualism is closely related to the fourth, which can perhaps best be seen if we now introduce a criticism that has been made of the third objection. This criticism can be stated as follows: James may be right that those Intellectualists are wrong who hold out for, say, absolute proof in cases where any reasonable person would be satisfied with just fairly strong evidence. But this has nothing to do with the case where the *only* evidence in favor of a proposition is the bare possibility that it could conceivably be true. We can legitimately run the risk of error in the first case, says the critic, but to do so in the second would be sheer foolishness.[16]

However, this criticism does not seem to me even to touch James's argument, for, as we will see, James is limiting his argument to those cases where (1) "the truth cannot be known" because the evidence is ambiguous (a case (3) kind of evidence-situation), and where (2) we *must* decide. And this constitutes James's final and most important objection to Intellectualism: that this view is completely unhelpful and is unable to guide us in those cases where we cannot wait, where we must choose, and where evidence is unavailable or is so meager that it cannot help us decide. In such a case, it cannot be called "foolishness" to exercise our choice, for the situation is such that we *must* decide.

Of James's four criticisms of Intellectualism, only the fourth is necessary to the development of his "right to believe" argument. The other objections might be fallacious and James's argument can still be sound. Consequently, only the fourth objection need concern us further here, and it will have to be examined in some detail.

James concludes, then, that Intellectualism cannot be the proper epistemological attitude in all evidence-situations. There are circumstances in which "believe truth" takes priority over "avoid error." That is to say, the will or passional nature is epistemologically justified in determining whether or not to believe a given proposition, where the evidence for and against the proposition is ambiguous and where the chance to gain the truth would be lost were the decision not made on passional grounds.

But there is an obvious objection to this: Can a person believe *any* proposition, however ludicrous, simply because his passional nature desires to embrace it, or because it might conceivably be true and he does not want to run the risk of losing the possibility of finding the truth? I have already anticipated James's negative answer. He felt that belief in nonevident propositions is warranted only in a certain kind of situation, and he describes this situation with some care.

James calls this situation a *genuine option*, by which he means an option that is "live," "forced," and "momentous." When we first read "The Will to Believe" and discover these Jamesian criteria of a "genuine option," we are immediately suspicious that there are difficulties and ambiguities involved in each. Later we shall have to examine each criterion carefully in order to determine (1) what James actually means in each case, (2) to what extent the distinctions he makes are sound and helpful distinctions, and (3) whether or not all the criteria he lists are actually necessary to his "right to believe" argument. However, for now I propose to accept the criteria at face value and explain them on as simple a level as possible. The questions and difficulties will be raised later.

We must first notice that James uses the term *option* in two different senses: an option either can be a situation in which a choice has to be made between two or more alternatives or can be one of the alternative choices. If a waitress in a restaurant says, "For dessert we have either ice cream or pie," the whole situation can be called an option to the extent that it calls for a real choice on the part of the customer, but "ice cream" can also be called one of the (two) options. Along with James, I will mainly use the term *option* in the first sense, for this is the sense that is clearly intended in the term *genuine option*, but I will occasionally use it in the second sense as well.

It is essential to notice that an option must meet *four* criteria—not three—in order to satisfy all the requirements of James's "right to believe" doctrine. (In "The Will to Believe," James calls any option *genuine* that satisfies the first three, but he is also careful to add the fourth before bringing in the "right to believe" doctrine. Since it will perhaps simplify matters, I will call an option genuine only if it satisfies all four criteria. This means that a genuine option is one to which the "right to believe" doctrine will apply.)

(1)   The option must be live.
(2)   The option must be momentous.
(3)   The option must be forced.
(4)   The option must not be decidable on intellectual grounds.

(1)   The option must be live. When a person must choose between the two alternatives (or options) of an option, they can be either live or dead to him. A live option is one that appeals to him as a distinct possibility, while a dead option is one that he has no inclination to accept. Believing in the Mahdi (a nineteenth-century Muslim military and religious

leader), James says, is a live option to an Arab, but dead to a non-Arab.

(2)   The option must be momentous rather than trivial. A momentous option is one in which something unique is offered that will be irrevocably lost if rejected, while a trivial option is insignificant in that the thing offered is not unique: it may perhaps be accepted or gained at a later date. "Come with me now on my expedition to the North Pole," James says, is momentous, for the opportunity to see the North Pole will probably never come again. But "Come with me now to the drug store" is clearly trivial. We can go to the drug store whenever we wish.

(3)   The option must be forced, not avoidable. A forced option is a dilemma based on a perfect disjunction in which a person *must* choose one of the two alternatives: there is no middle ground. An avoidable option, on the other hand, is one in which choice is not necessary. "Either call my theory true or call it false," James says, is an avoidable option, for we can remain indifferent to the proposed theory; that is, we can refuse to call it true and refuse to call it false. But "Either accept this truth or go without it" is forced: there is no middle ground, and so of necessity one of the two options must be chosen. For to decide not to choose, to decide to remain indifferent, is in itself a choice to go without the truth.

(4)   The option must be one that "the intellect of the individual cannot by itself resolve."[17] By this I take James to mean that the evidence must be ambiguous as to which of the two alternatives of the option is the more probable. (Accordingly, I will call this the *ambiguity criterion*.) Obviously, where the truth *can* be settled on evidential grounds, for example, in determining which disjunct is true in the proposition "New York is either north or south of Philadelphia," the "right to believe" doctrine is irrelevant. Whenever conclusive evidence is available, it takes precedence and decides the case. James's fourth criterion, then, is that whatever evidence is available must be inconclusive as to whether or not a given alternative is true or as to which alternative is the more probable. (And this is why I said earlier that in

"The Will to Believe" James is mainly interested in propositions that fit evidence-situation case 3.)

The point of these distinctions is that (1) in dead, avoidable, or trivial options the attitude of Intellectualism in order to avoid error is the only attitude that is epistemologically justified; and (2) in options that can be settled on evidential grounds the "right to believe" doctrine is not applicable. But, says James, in the unique case of genuine option—and only in this case—we are justified in believing as our will or passional nature directs. With full epistemological justification, we can choose (on the basis of our hopes or needs or wishes) to believe any proposition that is one of the alternative options of a genuine option. Of course, this does not necessarily mean that the proposition is true; the whole point of the ambiguity requirement is that it is yet unknown whether or not the proposition is true; it simply means that we are justified in affirming it. Only further testing will show whether or not the proposition is true, and when this is shown, the "right to believe" doctrine will no longer apply.

This, then, is the doctrine of "the right to believe." It should be quite clear that James has not said that we can believe anything we like or even that we can believe anything we like on an undecided issue. Anybody who thinks that this is James's thesis has not read "The Will to Believe" carefully enough. Thus R. B. Perry says:[18]

> James . . . was accused of encouraging *wilfulness* or *wanton[n]ess* of belief, or of advocating belief for belief's sake, whereas his whole purpose had been to justify belief. . . . His critics had accused him of advocating *license* in belief, whereas, on the contrary, his aim had been to formulate rules for belief.

However, it may be that the careless way James occasionally expressed his thesis, especially in the concluding section of "The Will to Believe," may have contributed to misunderstanding:[19]

> We have the right to believe at our own risk any hypothesis that is live enough to tempt our will. . . . The freedom to believe can only cover living options which the intellect of the individual cannot by itself resolve; and living options never seem absurdities to him who has them to consider.

And perhaps some of James's defenders unwittingly fostered confusion about his thesis as well. For example, even such a normally reliable interpreter as Perry, whom I just quoted in an attempt to correct this very misunderstanding, says:[20]

> James was from the beginning aware that belief serves two masters, theory and life. We are justified in believing what it is *desirable* or *right to believe*. These two justifications do not always coincide, there being an excess sometimes on one side, sometimes on the other. The case in which there is an excess of practical over theoretical justification is the case of "the right to believe."

Perry no doubt means that in those cases where there is *no* theoretical justification for believing, say, p over q, practical considerations must come into play if we are to decide between them, and if the option is forced, we must decide. This interpretation of Perry's words is entirely harmonious with James's "right to believe" doctrine. But unfortunately Perry's words can also be taken in another way: they can be taken to mean that in a case where p is theoretically justified (there is more evidence for p than for q), practical considerations may outweigh the theoretical and thus justify acceptance of q over p. This is not what James is saying in "The Will to Believe," for this interpretation entirely ignores the ambiguity requirement.

As I mentioned earlier, it will be necessary to investigate carefully the four criteria of genuineness. For we shall discover (1) interpreters of James who do not understand his "right to believe" doctrine because they fail to grasp one or another of his four criteria, and (2) critics of James whose criticisms are based on ignoring one or another of the criteria. Let us then turn to an investigation of each of the four criteria.

N O T E S

1. William James, *The Will To Believe and Other Essays in Popular Philosophy* (New York: Dover Publications, 1956). As well as "The Will To Believe," this volume also contains "The Sentiment of Rationality" and "Is Life Worth Living?". (Hereafter abbreviated as TWTB, SR, and ILWL.

2. Ralph Barton Perry, *The Thought and Character of William James* (Boston: Little, Brown, and Co., 1935), 2:243–48; Robert W. Beard, " 'The Will To Believe' Revised," *Ratio* 7 (December 1966) :170.

3. For example, Dickenson Miller, in his early critical essay, wrote: "The interpretation of the author's thesis that I gave at the outset seems no more than is implied in the title he has chosen for his book and such other expressions as were cited." " 'The Will To Believe' And The Duty To Doubt," *International Journal of Ethics* 9 (1898–99) :182. See also Miller's later essay, "James's Doctrine of 'The Right To Believe,' " *The Philosophical Review* 51 (1942) .

4. TWTB, pp. 8–11, 14, 18, 21.

5. W. K. Clifford, "The Ethics of Belief," *Lectures and Essays,* ed. Leslie Stephens and Frederick Pollack (New York: Macmillan and Company, 1901), 2:186.

6. *The Journal of Philosophy* 55 (1958) :578–88.

7. William James, *Some Problems of Philosophy: A Beginning of An Introduction To Philosophy* (New York: Longmans, Green, and Co., 1911), pp. 221–23. I will hereafter abbreviate this essay as FATRTB.

8. ILWL, p. 54.

9. Ibid., p. 56; cf. TWTB, p. 27.

10. FATRTB, pp. 224–25; cf. Ralph B. Perry, *In the Spirit of William James* (Bloomington: Indiana University Press, 1958), pp. 178–79, 196–97.

11. SR, p. 96; cf. TWTB, p. 11 and SR, pp. 90–91.

12. TWTB, pp. 10, 19; SR, pp. 92, 89.

13. SR, p. 91.

14. TWTB, p. 28; cf. SR, pp. 94–95 n. 1.

15. TWTB, p. 27.

16. See Walter Kaufmann, *Critique of Religion and Philosophy* (Garden City, N.Y.: Doubleday and Co., Inc., 1961), p. 116.

17. TWTB, p. 29; cf. p. 11.

18. Ralph B. Perry, *The Thought and Character of William James,* Briefer Version (New York: Harper and Row, 1948), p. 215.

19. TWTB, p. 29.

20. *In the Spirit,* p. 172.

6

The Criteria of Genuineness

In this chapter I will examine the four criteria of genuineness. I will try to discover as best I can what James meant in each case, and I will also try to come to grips with whatever difficulties each criterion faces. For despite the fact that the distinctions James makes seem clear at first reading, they raise a great many problems. I will try to resolve some of these difficulties, but some I will leave alone—especially those which do not appear to be of major importance in James's overall argument. Finally, I will also examine the question of the relationship between the four criteria; that is, I will try to see to what extent they depend on each other and to what extent each is really needed by James.

The Criterion of Liveness. Let us suppose that some hypothesis h is proposed to us. This hypothesis can be either live or dead, James says. It will be live if it tempts my belief, if its truth appeals to me as a distinct possibility, if I might be willing to bet on it. There appear to be two conditions here:

(1) h is live to me if h appears to me to be possibly true;[1] and

(2) h is live to me if I have an inclination to accept h, if h

"makes some appeal, however small" to my belief, if I have a "preexisting tendency to believe" h.[2]

James probably fails to distinguish between the two conditions because we are normally tempted to believe propositions that seem to us to be true. But this need not necessarily be the case. We often encounter propositions that we know may possibly be true, but that do not tempt our belief in the slightest. "My house will be robbed next week" is a proposition that *may* be true, but I have no inclination or preexisting tendency to believe it. Thus there are propositions which satisfy the first condition but not the second. And as we shall see presently, this gets James into difficulty in his example of the Mahdi, whose claims, he says, are live to Arabs but dead to non-Arabs. In addition, James tells us that there is a simple test to find out whether a given hypothesis is live or dead to a given person. It is his willingness to act on the hypothesis—by which I take James to mean his willingness to act on *the assumption of the truth of* the hypothesis, for example, by betting on it. Hypothesis h is a live hypothesis to anyone who is willing to act on h, dead to anyone who is not so willing. Again, I may purchase a new lock for my front door, but this would typically be an act based on the belief that "My house *may* be robbed," not the belief that "My house will be robbed."

This can now be applied to the concept of an option. An option will be live, James says, if its alternative hypotheses are both live; dead, if one or both of its alternative hypotheses are dead.

One apparent result of the liveness criterion is that James's "right to believe" argument will apply only to people who have not yet made up their minds on the matter of religion. It seems to follow that James's argument can never be used by a committed religious believer to justify his belief (nor, for that matter, by a committed atheist to justify *his* belief), for to the typical believer irreligion is not a live hypothesis (nor, to the atheist, is religion a live hypothesis). Of course, a religious believer might *claim* that atheism is a live option to him—a live option he happens to reject—and thus still attempt to use the "right to believe" to justify his faith. But then we could use James's test to find out whether or not the believer is being truthful with us. That is, we could simply ask him to what extent he is willing to act on the assumption of the truth of atheism—stop going to church, stop praying, or the like. And of course our believer will not be willing to do so, and so the "right to believe" cannot be used to justify his faith. (I will return to this point in chapter 9).

James would not consider this a serious difficulty, however, for he was probably directing his argument in "The Will to Believe" at people who were sitting on the fence anyway. But it does raise some questions about his "willingness to act" test. For, as with our believer, it does not seem to me that people are often willing to act on the assumption of the truth of a hypothesis they reject. We can imagine situations in which this might occur—"All right, just to keep you happy I'll take my umbrella, but I still do not think it is going to rain"—but these seem far from what James intends by the liveness criterion. It follows either that there is something wrong with James's test, or that no rejected hypothesis can ever be live.

The most serious difficulty with the liveness criterion is the subjectivity it implies. James himself admits that what is live to one person may be dead to another, and surely (we want to say) the question of whether a hypothesis is live or dead to a person has no bearing whatsoever on whether or not that person is justified in affirming it. For example, John Hick criticizes James as follows:[3]

> Whether or not belief constitutes a "live option" to a particular mind has no bearing upon its truth or falsity. All sorts of accidental circumstances may predispose us towards a proposition; the mere fact that is widely held in the society around us is often sufficient. . . . But it would clearly be absurd to suppose that the truth varies geographically with the liveliness of the local options. If we

are rational, then, and have been convinced by *The Will To Believe*, the mere thought of what might be gained if a proposition is true will automatically render it a live option to us, in whatever part of the world we may happen to live. Thus the example which James offers of a thoroughly dead option (the Mahdi and his offer of salvation to his followers) is an instance of one which his own argument, if sound, should bring to life in any thoughtful mind. . . . I do not see how James could consistently refuse [the Mahdi's] invitation. For if it is rational to believe in the Christian God on the ground that this *may* be the only way of gaining the final truth, then it is equally rational to believe in any alternative religious system which *may* also be the sole pathway to Truth. The fact that our minds are more accustomed to one claim than the other is an irrelevancy.

But I believe that Hick is mistaken in interpreting James. He takes the "right to believe" doctrine to be an argument about the truth and falsity of propositions, while it is actually an argument about the propriety of believing propositions whose truth value is unknown. It is true that all kinds of accidental factors that have no bearing whatsoever on a proposition's truth value are relevant to determining whether a proposition is live or dead to a given person. And if James were saying that the liveness or deadness of a hypothesis had some bearing on its truth value, he would clearly be open to Hick's criticism. But James is *not* saying that "the truth varies geographically with the liveliness of the local options." James does claim that believing an unproved proposition may be a way of gaining a truth we would have missed had we failed to believe it, but this is not to say that the truth depends on what is live or dead to a given person.

Returning now to the two conditions of liveness mentioned earlier, it is unclear whether the category of dead hypotheses includes only those hypotheses in which neither condition is satisfied or also includes those in which only one is satisfied. Clearly, a hypothesis that neither tempts me nor seems to me possibly true is dead for James: but what about a hypothesis that tempts me but that does not seem to me possibly true? Or what about one that seems to me possibly true but does not tempt me? James would probably call these hypotheses dead, but this is unclear.

This is where I believe that James gets into difficulty on his example of the Mahdi. Hick is right that if the claims James puts into the mouth of the Mahdi are momentous, that is, if they offer something important and unique—as they surely seem to—they ought to be live even to non-Arabs.[4] The problem here is that Hick's argument is undoubtedly correct as regards the second condition of liveness, but not necessarily correct as regards the first. That is, Hick is right that if a hypothesis is momentous to a given person, it ought to tempt his belief. But it does not follow that a momentous hypothesis must be one that seems possibly true.

Thus, if a hypothesis is killed when only one of the two conditions is not satisfied for it, Hick's argument that a momentous hypothesis should be live would be true only of a hypothesis that (1) was momentous, (2) seemed possibly true, and (3) did not tempt belief. But it would not necessarily be true of a hypothesis that (1) was momentous, (2) tempted belief, but (3) did not seem possibly true.

The Criterion of Momentousness. James's discussion of the momentousness criterion is brief and typically vivid:[5]

If I were Dr. Nansen and proposed to you to join my North Pole expedition, your option would be momentous; for this would probably be your only similar opportunity, and your choice now would either exclude you from the North Pole sort of immortality altogether or put at least the chance of it into your hands. He who refuses to embrace a unique opportunity loses the prize as surely as if he tried and failed. *Per contra,* the option is trivial when the opportunity is not unique, when the stake is insignificant, or when the decision is reversible if it later proves unwise.

There are three conditions here. An option is momentous if at least one of its alternatives is

(3) unique
(4) important
(5) irreversible

And an option will be trivial if any of these three conditions is not satisfied for at least one of its alternatives. (James does not say that only *one* of the alternatives must fulfill these conditions, but his example clearly implies it: in an option between going to the North Pole and not going to the North Pole, a decision not to go to the North Pole would surely not qualify as a momentous alternative.)

The first condition requires that there be at least a reasonably high probability that one of the alternatives will not occur again. There is a very high probability that I will be able to go to the drugstore again, and so "Come with me now to the drugstore" is a trivial alternative. In order to satisfy condition (3), then, the alternative must offer a unique opportunity that will be irrevocably lost if rejected. Condition (4) requires that at least one of the alternatives be of great importance to me; a "high stake" and a sense of urgency must be involved. If at this moment it doesn't particularly matter to me whether or not I go to the drugstore, then "Come with me now to the drugstore" is a trivial option. (Here again the subjectivity we saw in the liveness criterion becomes evident; for surely what is important to Jones at one time may be unimportant to Smith at the same time or even to Jones at a later time.) Finally, condition (5) requires that at least one of the alternatives be one on which, when a decision is made, that decision will be irreversible. That is, the decision must be one that I cannot later change if it proves unwise or if I have a change of heart. If I refuse Dr. Nansen's invitation to join his polar expedition, I cannot later change my mind—not, at least, after the expedition has departed. Thus Dr. Nansen's "Come with me now to the North Pole" is a momentous alternative.

Condition (4) is clear enough and presents no additional difficulties, but (3) and (5) raise some questions. The problem with the uniqueness condition is that in a sense *all* options present unique opportunities, for no two options are exactly alike. In a sense, every decision we ever make is momentous, for no decision uniquely like it will ever come up again. Even "Come with me now to the drugstore" is unique because of the "now," for if the opportunity passes to go *now* to the drugstore (i.e., at a given fleeting moment in time), it will never again arise. However, I do not believe that this objection presents serious dfficulties for James, for he can call our attention to the phrase "This would be your only *similar* opportunity" (italics added) in the extract just quoted above. Thus James could argue that a unique opportunity is one about which it could be said that nothing *significantly* or *relevantly* like it will ever occur again. It would then be a fairly easy matter to spell out what the "relevant similarities" are and show why many opportunities relevantly similar to "Come with me now to the drugstore" will probably present themselves again, while no opportunity relevantly similar to "Come with me now to the North Pole" will probably ever occur again.

The difficulty with the irreversibility condition had been pointed out by Beard:[6]

The stipulation that in addition a decision must not be reversible is puzzling. If this requirement is to be more than a mere pleonasm, it must not mean simply that the opportunity offered by one of the alternatives is unique and important. Rather, it should mean that once we have committed ourselves to a belief, we could not backslide even if we later discover to our dismay that the decision was unwise. There are, of course, some conceivable courses of action that are irreversible in this way. E.g., an accomplished murder may result from earlier choice, and does not offer us an opportunity for reversal. For that matter, any decision once it becomes a *fait accompli* is irreversible in the same way provided that the world is in some measure affected by the decision. So what James must intend is that the decision cannot be reversible prior to its confirmation or prior to some specified effects resulting from the fact that someone holds a particular belief. But it is surely difficult to imagine what choice would have this property. Surely one might abandon an optimistic view of the world, or the belief that one has a particular moral obligation, or that a previously chosen religious hypothesis will be confirmed. Perhaps the example that would come nearest to satisfying the condition as James states it would be a deathbed conversion, but this can hardly be what he has in mind.

The problem here is an apparent ambiguity in the irreversibility condition. On the one hand, it is clear that the "right to believe" doctrine is a doctrine about *beliefs,* but on the other hand the irreversibility condition seems mainly applicable to *actions.* It is true that decisions about courses of action can be irreversible, and in the passage quoted in chapter 6 in which James introduces the momentousness criterion it is obviously decisions about actions that he is talking about and not beliefs. But surely Beard is correct that only in extreme cases can we imagine what it would be like for a belief to be irreversible. It may be that James could try to save himself at this point by arguing that beliefs are what lead to actions, that actions are explainable in terms of beliefs— which is what he does hold anyway (I shall consider this point in chapter 7). But this will not solve the problem, for even if they are closely (even causally) related, it is still true that beliefs are not actions, and since the "right to believe" doctrine is a doctrine about beliefs, it is hard to see how the irreversibility condition belongs in the doctrine.

If this reasoning is sound, it would also appear that the uniqueness condition is in trouble too. For it can be argued that this condition also applies less to beliefs than to actions or opportunities for action. James might claim that it is not difficult to see how a belief could be unique, but it could then be pointed out that when James gets around to showing how religion offers us a momentous option, it is not so much religious beliefs themselves that are supposed to be unique as what the beliefs are in, that is, what is offered to us in religion. It would appear then, that there are serious difficulties connected with both the uniqueness and the irreversibility conditions of the momentousness criterion.

The Criterion of Forcedness. An option is avoidable if it faces a person with a choice that need not be made because of the presence of another alternative. "Choose either a or b" is an avoidable option if it is possible to avoid the offered choice by instead choosing c. Thus, James says, "Either call my theory true or call it false" is an avoidable option, for there is a third alternative, namely, remaining indifferent, neither calling the theory true nor calling it false. An option is forced if it faces a person with a dilemma based on a perfect disjunction, with a choice that *must* be made because there is no third alternative. "Choose either a or b" is a forced option if no other choice is available than a or b. Thus James says, "Either accept this truth or go without it" is a forced option; there is no third alternative. For even if a decision is made not to choose, that is, to remain indifferent, this in itself would constitute a choice of "going without it."

The reason for this is that the consequences would be the same. To use a common example, suppose I come home to find my house on fire. I do not know whether or not my children are in the house, and no one else is nearby to help me. I am then faced with a forced option: either I shall enter the house to rescue my children or I shall not. There is no third alternative, for if I decide not to decide, if I decide to refuse to choose between the two alternatives, the result will be exactly the same had I decided not to enter the house, that is, I will not enter the house. And if it turns out that my children *are* in the house, they will die unrescued.

As Beard points out, James is actually working with two conditions here. An option will be forced if its alternatives

(6)   are mutually exclusive, and
(7)   exhaust all the possibilities.

The difficulty here is with condition 7. For it seems that with a few verbal changes *any* option can be stated in such a way as to exhaust all the possibilities, and this seems to trivialize the whole concept of a forced option. Thus "Either call my theory true or call it false," James's own example of an avoidable option, can be formulated as "Either call my theory true or do not call it true," which is forced. And "Either believe in God or deny that he exists" can be formulated as the forced option, "Either believe in God or do not believe in God." Thus, to satisfy the exhaustiveness condition, it appears that all we need is a certain ability to manipulate words.

Beard suggests that the forcedness criterion can be saved only by abandoning the exhaustiveness condition. He points out that the two conditions listed above do not require that there be only two alternatives, but just that the alternatives be mutually exclusive and exhaust all the possibilities. He says:[7]

> It is somewhat surprising in view of the possibility of several alternatives that James should insist on the exhaustiveness requirement. It appears sufficient that the alternatives exclude one another and that each be live. One may, e.g., be tempted to become a Mohammedan and at the same time be tempted by Christianity. Assume for the moment that these alternatives are exclusive and that agnosticism, atheism, and other possible alternatives are not in the least tempting. The option could not, then, be genuine because it would not be justified, no matter how urgent the decision may seem. . . . We may attempt to salvage the notion of a forced option by abandoning the requirement that the alternatives be logically exhaustive. Let an option be forced whenever the alternatives are mutually exclusive, and exhaustive of the tempting beliefs, though not logically exhaustive.

However, perhaps there is a way that the exhaustiveness condition can be saved. I shall try to save it by arguing against the claim that we can logically convert any option into a forced option by wording it differently. For it seems to me that an avoidable option verbally "converted" into a forced option is really a *different* option from what it was before. Thus to take the two options "Either call my theory true or call it false" (avoidable) and "Either call my theory true or do not call it true" (forced), I would deny that these options are the same. They are similar in some ways, of course, but one is still a very different option from the other, and so to "convert" one into the other—if that is the right word— is really to create an entirely new and different option. Similarly, "Either believe in God or deny that he exists" (avoidable) is a very different option from "Either believe in God or do not believe in God" (forced). It is true that with a few verbal changes we can thus pass from an avoidable option to a forced option, but this should not surprise us, for with a few verbal changes any expression that can be put into words can be changed into something that sounds similar but says something different. The real question to ask of a person in an evidence-situation, then, is not "Can your option be changed into a forced option with a few verbal changes?", but, "Is the option you are now actually confronted with forced or avoidable?" We should not try to change the option that the person faces but rather understand it.

So to "reformulate" an avoidable option into a forced option is not really a matter of *reformulating* the old option but of capriciously creating a different one altogether. Nor will it "satisfy" the exhaustiveness condition to change a person's avoidable option into a forced option, for this will create an option that the person is not actually facing. It will be an artificially contrived choice—not the real choice he actually faces.

The important question, then, is whether or not people actually do face options that exhaust all the possibilities. Perhaps not often, but it seems to me that they sometimes do, for example, the person who wonders whether or not to enter the burning house, the person who wonders whether or not to run for political office, the person who wonders whether or not to become a Christian. It is true that the person who faces this last option may well face another too: Shall I become a Christian or an atheist? This is a different option from the first, and since it is not forced, the "right to believe" doctrine will not apply to it. So, again, in deciding whether or not a given evidence-situation is one in which the "right to believe" doctrine can be invoked, the real question is, What kind of option is the person actually facing? It may be that only the person himself could tell us this for sure—"But you see I'm not worried about atheism: what I need to decide is whether or not to become a Christian"— but this will not affect the validity of the exhaustiveness condition itself.

An entirely different point about the forcedness criterion is raised by George Mavrodes, and it will force us to refine our understanding of the criterion slightly. He suggests that the forcedness criterion makes superfluous James's argument about the "believe truth" rule's taking priority over the "avoid error" rule. For "it was the usual possibility of non-commitment which gave the distinction [between the two rules] its validity. . . . But where the possibility of remaining uncommitted disappears, as it must in the forced options, there the distinction vanishes too."[8]

Now I do not believe that this issue will turn out to be crucial, for I do not think that the "right to believe" doctrine ultimately needs the business about the two rules, as I shall argue in chapter 9. However, I do not agree that the forcedness criterion makes the distinction between the two rules pointless, for I think that this conclusion is based on a misunderstanding of the criterion. As we have seen, James says that in a forced option there is "no possibility of not choosing." The problem is that there are two ways these words can be interpreted. The first interpretation is this: whenever a person is faced with a forced option between a and b, he must choose one or the other alternative, that is, he *must make a conscious choice* for either a or b. The second interpretation looks similar only at first glance: Whenever a person is faced with a forced option between a and b, *whatever he does, even if it is not choosing, it will constitute a choice* of either a or b.

The first interpretation must be rejected. It is not only inherently implausible, but it is clearly contrary to James's intentions. For at the conclusion of "The Will to Believe," where he speaks of the person who wants to suspend judgment and wait till coercive evidence is available on the forced option that James calls "the religious hypothesis," James says, "Indeed we *may* wait if we will,—I hope you do not think I am denying that,—but if we do so, we do so at our peril as much as if we believed. In either case we *act,* taking our life into our hands."[9] So James is not saying that in the case of a forced option a conscious choice of one of the alternatives must be made. We *can* suspend judgment: it is just that *in effect,* that is, in its consequences, this choice will constitute a choice of one of the alternatives.

Perhaps we might make the following distinction: in the case of a forced option suspension of judgment is psychologically possible but pragmatically impossible. It is psychologically possible because, after all, no one hypnotizes or coerces the decider into making an actual choice of one of the alternatives. So he *can* say: "I suspend judgment on whether to believe in God or not to believe in God." But suspension of judgment is pragmatically impossible in a forced option because it does not "escape the issue"; its consequences will be identical to those of an actual choice of one of the alternatives. In effect, suspension of judgment will constitute a choice of one of the alternatives.

We can now see how James's argument about the two rules fits into his overall strategy. As regards the "will to believe" doctrine, which we will consider later, it can be seen that anyone who gives priority to the "avoid error" rule will (because of his unwillingness to commit himself to nonevident propositions) fail to discover the truth in those cases where faith is self-verifying. But anyone who gives priority to the "believe truth" rule will be willing to commit himself to belief and will discover the truth in those same areas. In these areas, then, it is clear that the "believe truth" rule ought to take priority.

As regards the "right to believe" doctrine, James's argument that the "believe truth" rule takes priority can be seen as designed to prevent people from suspending judgment in forced options. As we have seen, we *can* suspend judgment in forced options, but such an attitude is foolish. For the person who suspends judgment thinks he is avoiding choice, but he has actually made a choice. It is the desire to avoid error that motivates the attitude of suspended judgment, and in the case of most options, avoiding error can be guaranteed by suspending judgment. But in the case of a forced option this is not true. In effect, suspension of judgment constitutes a choice of one of the alternatives; whatever we do, it will constitute a decision. Thus there is no longer any reason to hold that the "avoid error" rule takes priority. And anyone who sees this will no longer be tempted to suspend judgment in forced options. Thus Mavrodes is wrong when he argues that the distinction between the two rules has no point in cases of forced options. I conclude, then, that the forcedness criterion stands.

The Ambiguity Criterion. In his later essay,[10] Dickinson Miller claims that "The Will to Believe" cannot be understood apart from one of the cardinal principles of James's empiricism, namely, the principle that "there is no test of truth." (This is the same point that Sextus makes in his denial that there is a "criterion of truth.") It is true that James makes this point both in "The Will to Believe" and elsewhere: "No bell in us tolls to let us know for certain when the truth is in our grasp," "No concrete test of what is really true has ever been agreed upon." Thus "objective certainty" is never to be had; evidence that is absolutely and indubitably conclusive is not to be found. We can never know that we know.[11]

Miller argues that James needs this doctrine if his argument is to succeed, and argues further that the doctrine is unsound. Now it is true that James also seems to think that this doctrine is necessary to "The Will to Believe," for he implies that if we had an infallible criterion of truth the attitude of waiting till the bell tolls would always be the proper attitude; it is the absence of the truth bell that makes voluntary choice ahead of the evidence necessary.[12]

However, despite both James and Miller, it does not seem to me that the "right to believe" argument needs this doctrine at all. Contrary to the connection James draws between the absence of a criterion and the need to choose, it seems to me that it is the fact that the option is forced, rather than the absence of a criterion, that makes choice necessary. It may be that in all *avoidable* options James would be right that, were there a criterion of truth, the attitude of postponing choice till the bell tolls would be justified. But in the case of a forced option, the whole point is that we pragmatically *cannot* postpone decision: for to decide not to choose is itself a tacit choice of one of the alternatives.

So James does not need the doctrine that "there is no test of truth" for his "right to believe" doctrine to succeed, and if the first doctrine is unsound (I do not claim that it is), this does not necessarily mean that the second is unsound. All he needs, I think, is that there be options the acceptability of whose alternatives cannot be settled on intellectual (i.e., evidential) grounds. Obviously, where the truth *can* be settled on evidential grounds, for example, in determining the acceptability of the proposition "New York is north of Philadelphia," the "right to believe" doctrine has no relevance whatsoever. When conclusive evidence is available, it takes precedence.

The ambiguity criterion is satisfied in those cases where the available evidence is "insufficient," where "doubt is still theoretically possible," where to believe a proposition would amount to "going beyond the literal evidence," where "our mere logical intellect may or may not have been coerced," where there is no objective "proof" or "evidence" because all the evidence is not yet "in," where the proposition in question is one for which "there is no outward proof," one that cannot be "refuted or proved by logic" or "be decided on intellectual grounds." It applies in those cases where we must decide now and cannot wait for "sensible proof" or "till objective evidence comes in" or till "coercive evidence shall have arrived."[13]

It is important to note James's own words here, for despite his many ways of making what seems like a relatively simple point—namely, that the question must be one on which the evidence is ambiguous—there is still some residual unclarity. For we can imagine several kinds of situations where it might be claimed that the evidence is ambiguous on the truth or falsity of a proposition p.

(8) No evidence is now available or ever will be available relative to the truth or falsity of p.

(9) No evidence is now available relative to the truth or falsity of p and there will probably never be any.

(10) No evidence is now available relative to the truth or falsity of p but at some time in the future evidence will probably be available.

(11) No sufficient, adequate, coercive evidence is now available relative to the truth or falsity of p. There is only a slight preponderance of evidence for p over not-p (or vice-versa).

(12) The evidence for p and against not-p is evenly balanced with the evidence for not-p and against p, i.e., the evidence for p and against not-p is neither stronger nor weaker than the evidence for not-p and against p.

Let us call "the ambiguity problem" (1) the problem of deciding what James actually meant here, and (2) aside from what he meant, the problem of deciding which of the above situations will make the "right to believe" doctrine work and which will not. The "will to believe" doctrine seems best to fit in cases where evidence is only presently absent, for James's point is that a commitment of faith ahead of the evidence will create confirming evidence later. But with the "right to believe" doctrine, it is obvious that James never bothered to consider the above distinctions.

However, for now we need not press this question. For present purposes let us tentatively conclude that all that James needs to satisfy the ambiguity criterion is a proposition about which the available evidence is far from compelling or conclusive. There may or may not be relevant evidence available, but the point is that the situation must be such that a rational person acting only on the basis of the available evidence would be unable to make up his mind. Of course, if evidence is available, there is also the question of how ambiguous it actually has to be. Does the evidence for and against the two alternatives have to be exactly equal? But how could this be determined? Does it just have to be very close? And if so, how close? (I will return to this question in chapter 8.)

However, let us conclude that the ambiguity criterion requires that the option in question be one the truth or falsity of whose alternatives cannot be determined because the evidence that is available, if any is available, is not decisive enough to justify a choice based on the evidence alone. In other words, the evidence must be ambiguous on the truth or falsity of the alternatives. This may seem to include all five of the situations described above, but I do not think this need raise any difficulties for now.

Based on the conclusion that we have reached, it would seem that an option will now be genuine if and only if:

(13)   Both of its alternatives seem to be possibly true to the subject.

(14)   Both of its alternatives are appealing to the subject.

(15)   At least one of its alternatives is important to the subject.

(16)   Its alternatives are mutually exclusive.

(17)   Its alternatives exhaust all the possible choices.

(18)   The evidence is ambiguous on the truth or falsity of the alternatives.

However, it seems to me that when we consider what James is actually trying to accomplish by them, some of his criteria are superfluous. It will be recalled that in chapter 5 I concluded that James's most telling criticism of Intellectualism is that this view cannot help us in cases where we must decide between two alternatives and where evidence is unavailable or is so meager or ambiguous that it cannot help us decide. As I am interpreting James, this is precisely the kind of case as where he is arguing that Russell's Principle does not hold, where we can justifiably make a decision between two alternatives on some basis *other* than that of the available evidence.

I will call such a case a "Jamesian case." It occurs whenever

(19)   There is a forced option between two alternatives, i.e., the two alternatives are mutually exclusive and are exhaustive of all possible choices.

(20)   The evidence is ambiguous on the truth or falsity of the two alternatives.

I am saying, then, that James does not actually need the liveness and the momentousness criteria to make his "right to believe" argument work. For I am claiming that his doctrine amounts to a denial that Russell's Principle always holds, and it is precisely in a Jamesian case that James would want to claim that it does not hold and that we are therefore justified in believing as our passional nature directs. James does not need the first two criteria, for surely if an option is forced—we *must* decide—it does not matter whether or not it is also live or momentous. Thus the first criterion of the Jamesian case rules out the possibility of not choosing and the second rules out the possibility of choosing on the basis of evidence. All that is left, then, is to choose on some basis other than evidence—which is exactly what the doctrine of the "right to believe" is all about.

NOTES

1. TWTB, pp. 26, 27. Cf. also p. 29: "Living options never seem absurd to him who has them to consider."

2. TWTB, pp. 3, 6.

3. Hick, *Faith and Knowledge*, p. 43.

4. And thus James was wrong in saying to his readers, "If for any of you religion be a hypothesis that cannot, by any living possibility be true, then you need go no further." TWTB, p. 26. For if the claims of religion are momentous, James's irreligious readers *should* have considered them live.

5. TWTB, p. 4; see also pp. 19–20.

6. Beard, "'The Will To Believe' Revisited," p. 177.

7. Ibid., pp. 176–177. See also Kaufmann, p. 116.

8. George Mavrodes, "James and Clifford on 'The Will to Believe,'" *The Personalist* 44 (1963):194.

9. TWTB, p. 30.

10. Miller, "James's Doctrine of 'The Right to Believe,'" pp. 542–43, 551.

11. TWTB, pp. 30, 15; cf. pp. 14, 12.

12. TWTB, p. 30.

13. TWTB, p. 27; SR, pp. 90, 91; TWTB, pp. 1–2; SR, p. 107; TWTB, p. 25; SR, p. 91; TWTB, pp. 23, 11; cf. also SR, pp. 75–76, 91–92, 94–96; TWTB, pp. 29, 20, 22, 24.

7

Criticisms of James's Doctrine

"The Will to Believe" has been subjected to at least as many out-of-hand dismissals and careless denunciations as to reasoned criticisms. We need not deal with the former, but in this chapter we shall consider several substantive and important criticisms that have been made of the "right to believe" doctrine. Since my aim is to defend this doctrine, I shall try to show that each criticism can be successfully answered.

The first criticism focuses on the view of faith that James presupposes and tries to defend. The criticism is that the faith James is talking about has very little to do with the religious faith of the typical believer.[1] James defines faith as "a believing attitude in religious matters in spite of the fact that our merely logical intellect may not have been coerced," as "belief in something concerning which doubt is still theoretically possible," as "the readiness to act in a cause the prosperous issue of which is not certified to us in advance." "Faith," he says, "is synonymous with working hypothesis."[2]

The objection is that James seems to make faith into the kind of carefully considered gamble that a conniving skeptic might make. But surely (so this objection runs) judiciously weighing the evidence and tentatively deciding to risk acceptance of the working hypothesis "God exists" bears little relationship to the vital, living, certain faith of the religious believer. A working hypothesis is a supposition not actually believed but temporarily accepted in order to see what follows. But the believer wants to say that he *knows God.* He is absolutely certain; he does not even entertain the possibility that God might not exist. So it follows that his faith is anything but a working hypothesis. To guess (even correctly) that God exists is not to know God; to accept the working hypothesis that God exists is not to have faith in God; and to have decided that religious faith is epistemologically justified is not to have religious faith. Thus Santayana, in a famous comment, says: "There was accordingly no sense of security, no joy, in James' apology for personal religion. He did not really believe; he merely believed in the right of believing that you might be right if you believed."[3]

I believe that the proper response to this is to admit that the "faith" James is talking about is different from the faith of the religious believer. In the first place, let me duly record the fact that "The Will to Believe" is a work of philosophy of religion, not a description of religious experience. And if for the purposes of this essay James identifies faith with working hypothesis, he nowhere claims that this is *all* there is to religious faith. (James's effort in the way of describing religious experience is *The Varieties of Religious Experience;* it is difficult to understand how anyone who has read this work could argue that James reduces religious faith to working hypothesis.) So James is not claiming that the faith of the ordinary believer is like a scientific hypothesis, gambled upon prudently but tentatively. As part of his general epistemological argument of which religious faith is one application, he claims only that religious convictions held in this tentative kind of way are or can be epistemologically justified.

Second, as James himself notes,[4] it is important to understand the audience he was addressing in "The Will to Believe." (Like so many of James's short articles, it was originally a speech—in this case first delivered in 1895 to a combined meeting of the Philosophical Clubs of Yale and Brown Universities.) So it was not an audience of religious believers armed with the unshakable faith that Miller and Hick talk about; it was an audience of philosophers, many of whom no doubt had serious misgivings about religion. Perhaps there were some in his audience, James may have thought, who wanted to accept a religious outlook on life but who were prevented from doing so by their scientific and philosophical scruples. Thus it is understandable why James reasoned that for such a person it might be useful to refer to faith as a "working hypothesis." For this term is neutral vis-à-vis the truth of religion; and it expresses well the question such a person would face: Is holding a religious world view epistemologically justified or not? And again, James is not committed to the claim that "working hypothesis" is all there is to religious belief, for he could argue that the acceptance of such a hypothesis could later become a full-blown and unshakable faith.

Finally, and perhaps most important, it does not seem to me that the identification of faith with working hypothesis is crucial to the "right to believe" doctrine. The part that *is* crucial, because of the ambiguity criterion, is the injunction to retain an open mind in case further evidence later becomes available. For the doctrine holds only in cases where evidence is either absent or ambiguous; once evidence becomes unambiguous the doctrine can no longer be invoked. So it is incumbent upon the person whose religious belief is held on the basis of the "right to believe" doctrine to allow his belief to be modifiable by further evidence. (I shall return to this point in chapters 9 and 10.)

It might be objected at this point that James has still failed to describe the experience of the typical believer, for the believer precisely does *not* have an open mind. He is absolutely certain; nothing will or even conceivably could change his mind—which is the issue that was raised by Anthony Flew a few years ago in the "theology and falsification" debate.

But the answer to this is that it has not been shown that such an attitude on the part of the believer is justified. So if the critic takes this line against James, James could simply say, "Yes, I have failed to describe accurately the faith of the typical believer, to the extent that this faith involves irrational bliks. But the faith that I am defending, which is identical to the believer's faith except that it is held with an open mind to future evidence either pro or con, is preferable to the believer's faith."

Bertrand Russell's discussion of "The Will to Believe" in *A History of Western Philosophy*[5] is more puzzling than illuminating because it is based on an interpretation of James's essay that seems to be nothing but a cruel distortion. One almost feels that Russell did not bother to read the essay; he certainly failed to read it carefully. Beard points out several reasons for Russell's failure to understand the "right to believe" doctrine,[6] but perhaps the most important is his failure to grasp the criteria an option must satisfy in order to be genuine. However, Russell does make one criticism that is serious enough to consider, and that is that James has ignored the notion of probability in constructing the "right to believe" doctrine, and that the doctrine collapses once considerations of probability are brought in. That is, James argues as if complete belief or complete disbelief were the only two cognitive attitudes we can take toward a proposition, but this is obviously not true: there are all shades of doubt and belief. Furthermore, it is not true that if a person lacks firm conviction he will be indecisive and unable to act. It is entirely possible to act vigorously and decisively on a proposition that is known to possess only a degree of probability.

There are several things that need to be said in answer to this objection. The first is that it is true that in "The Will to Believe" James does not explicitly mention the notion of probability, but (1) the notion is implicitly present in at least three different ways, (2) James explicitly deals with the notion in another related essay, and (3) it is perhaps for a good reason that James did not emphasize probability in "The Will to Believe."

(1)   The notion of probability is present in the momentousness, liveness, and ambiguity criteria of a genuine option. The momentousness of an alternative will be determined in part by a judgment about its uniqueness, that is, a judgment as to the probability that what the alternative offers will ever be offered again. The liveness of an alternative is measured in part by our willingness to bet on it, which will be based on a judgment on our part as to the probability of its truth. And the ambiguity criterion, translated into the language of probability, requires either that the alternatives of the option be equal or very nearly equal in probability or else be such that a judgment of probability cannot be made about them.

(2)   James explicitly deals with the notion of probability in relation to religious faith in "Faith and the Right to Believe." He admits that we rarely have anything approaching absolute certainty and that in most emergencies we have to act on probability and run the risk of error. In many cases it is possible to determine *how* probable the occurrence of a given event is, and we can express this probability in terms of a fraction. For example, the probability that it will rain tomorrow may be .5. But the problem is that in most cases we cannot *act* fractionally. I could not very well take half my umbrella to work tomorrow: I must either take it or not take it. In many such cases, then, we must act wholly either for one alternative or for the other.

Most religious and metaphysical options are of this kind, James says. Here we cannot act fractionally: there must be "a certain wholeness in our faith." "To calculate the probabilities and act fractionally" (e.g., by one day adopting one metaphysical outlook and the next day another), he says, "would be to make the worst possible mess of it. Inaction also often counts as action."[7] So it can be seen that James is not arguing that there are always only two cognitive attitudes—acceptance or rejection—that we can adopt toward a proposition. He knows that there are shades of doubt and belief, and that we can act on propositions we know to be only probable. The point is, there are cases where, when it comes to *action,* we must either act as if we wholly accept a proposition or else act as if we wholly reject it. In the case of the proposition "It will rain today," I must either take my umbrella to work (indicating acceptance) or leave it at home (indicating rejection). And furthermore, we have already seen that, even if we accept a proposition on the basis of the "right to believe" doctrine, James stresses that we must retain an open mind for further evidence if it later becomes available. Thus, in a sense, even the "right to believe" doctrine itself is an example of what is supposedly missing in James, namely, acting on a proposition that is known to be only probable.

(3)   There are perhaps two reasons why James did not emphasize the notion of probability in "The Will to Believe": first, because we often cannot act fractionally, and second, because even when we speak of belief rather than action, in the "right to believe" doctrine James is limiting himself to "forced options" where, in effect, we cannot even *believe* fractionally.

Thus it is difficult to see why the "right to believe" doctrine must collapse, as Russell claims it must, once considerations of probability are raised.

The next objection is closely related to the last. Let me introduce it by noting an aspect of James's argument that I have not previously stressed, namely, the close connection he posits between belief and action. This point is not one that the reader of James's early essays might notice immediately, but James does make his position clear, and the point has a certain below-the-surface importance in the essays, as we shall see. Here are four passages where James speaks to this point:[8]

Deadness and liveness in an hypothesis are not intrinsic

properties, but relations to the individual thinker. They are measured by his willingness to act. The maximum of liveness in an hypothesis means willingness to act irrevocably. Practically, that means belief; but there is some believing tendency wherever there is willingness to act at all.

Since belief is measured by action, he who forbids us to believe religion to be true, necessarily also forbids us to act as we should if we did believe it to be true. The whole defense of religious faith hinges upon action. If the action required or inspired by the religious hypothesis is in no way different from that dictated by the naturalistic hypothesis, then religious faith is a pure superficiality, better pruned away. . . . I myself believe, of course, that the religious hypothesis gives to the world an expression which specifically determines our reactions, and makes them in a large part unlike what they might be on a purely naturalistic scheme of belief.

As the psychologists tell us, belief and doubt are living attitudes, and involve conduct on our part. Our only way, for example, of doubting, or refusing to believe, that a certain thing *is,* is continuing to act as if it were *not.*

The test of belief is willingness to act.

Matson has criticized James by arguing that belief cannot be equated with tendency to act.[9] There is a difference between a reasonable belief and a reasonable action, Matson says, and the "right to believe" doctrine is based on ignoring this distinction. Matson is willing to admit that in many evidence-situations sufficient evidence is lacking about what course of action to take, that it would be foolish therefore to refuse to act, and that action must accordingly be taken on the basis of weak evidence. But this kind of situation has to do with the rationality of actions, not of beliefs, he says, and belief cannot be identified with tendency to act.

In the first place, we know that what constitutes a rational act is different from what constitutes a rational belief because of cases like the following. (This is not Matson's example.) Let us suppose that a patient is dying of a certain disease. His doctor knows that if he prescribes a certain drug, the patient has a 10% chance of recovering, and he knows that there is no other known treatment for the disease. Here is a case where it would be rational for the doctor to *act,* that is, to prescribe the drug. But it would be foolish for the doctor, as a scientist, to *believe* that the drug will cure the patient, for the probabilities are far too low to justify such a belief. (For the patient's sake some people might claim it would be wise for the doctor to *pretend* to believe it, but that is another matter.) Here, then, is a case where, as regards belief, the doctor should "hedge his bets" and wait for more evidence.

And second, the same example shows that belief cannot be identified with tendency to act, for simply because the doctor prescribes the drug does not necessarily mean that he believes that the drug will cure the patient. Such action need only show his awareness of the (slight) possibility that the drug *might* cure the patient. What makes a belief reasonable, Matson says, is evidence in its favor; what makes an action reasonable is expediency. We can see, then, that there are cases where it would be reasonable (expedient) to act on an unreasonable (nonevident) belief. Matson then claims that the "right to believe" doctrine reduces to what I shall call "the pragmatic argument" (the argument that we are justified in holding a belief if holding the belief produces better practical consequences than not holding it). For the "right to believe" doctrine is now seen to urge that reasonable actions take priority over reasonable beliefs.

I shall consider the pragmatic argument and its relation to the "right to believe" doctrine next; for now, let us concentrate on the matter of belief and action. First of all, it is true that there are cases where we have to hedge our bets and wait for further evidence. James should not be taken as denying this. But since the "right to believe" doctrine is concerned with forced options, this point has no relevance to the doctrine. James is talking about cases where we must decide, where we cannot wait.

But as to the main point—Matson's attempt to separate belief from tendency to act, on the one hand I believe that it does not particularly matter who is right here for, as I shall argue in chapter 9, the "right to believe" doctrine can be stated without the identification of belief with tendency to act. But on the other hand, even if this identification is crucial, it does not seem to me that Matson has succeeded in making his case. For all he has shown is that the doctor's action in prescribing the drug cannot be identified with the particular belief that the drug will cure the patient; he has not shown that the action cannot be identified with any belief at all. Matson's own example is this: a man who comes home to find his house on fire and who enters the house to see if his children are inside is not necessarily of the belief that they are inside—he may just be checking. But Matson has not shown that the man's action cannot be identified with any belief at all. Indeed, Matson admits[10] that his action can be identified with the belief that the children *may* be inside the house, the belief that this is at least a possibility. Of course the belief "My children may be inside the house" is a different belief from "My children are inside the house," but it is still a belief.

Let us now turn to the matter of the relation of "The Will to Believe" to pragmatism. There are several issues here: (1) the historical issue of whether or not James's early essays helped form the foundation of his later, full-blown pragmatism; (2) the exegetical question of whether or not James used pragmatic arguments in his defense of religious faith in the early essays; and (3) the philosophical question of whether or not the "right to believe" doctrine needs pragmatic assumptions to succeed—either the pragmatic theory of truth or what I am calling "the pragmatic argument."

As I mentioned in chapter 5, there are interpreters of James who read the early essays in the light of his later pragmatism. Bertrand Russell thinks that pragmatism is an amplification of "The Will to Believe" and that it would be "unfair" to separate the two, and we have already encountered Matson's view that the "right to believe" doctrine reduces to the claim that on pragmatic grounds reasonable actions ought to take priority over reasonable beliefs.

Let us pause for a moment to clarify terms. Let us distinguish among three ways in which it might be claimed that a belief could be justified. By the "will to believe" doctrine, a belief is justified if it is self-verifying; by the "right to believe" doctrine, a belief is justified if it is an alternative of a genuine option; and by what I call "the pragmatic argument," a belief is justified if holding it leads to greater positive value for the believer and for others than would either disbelief or an alternative belief.

Two points are quite clear: first, the early essays did, in several ways, help lead James in the direction of pragmatism, and second, James does offer the pragmatic argument in defense of religious faith in several of his later writings. It should also be admitted that there are places in the early essays where James comes very near using the pragmatic argument in defense of religion. For example, in "Is Life Worth Living?" he says, "We have a right to believe the physical order to be only a partial order . . . we have a right to supplement it by an unseen spiritual order which we assume on trust, *if only thereby life may seem to us better worth living again.*"[11]

There are, then, places in the early essays where James's language can be interpreted as advancing arguments that can be called pragmatic arguments, but it still seems to me (1) that the pragmatic argument is a very different defense of faith from either the "right to believe" or the "will to believe" doctrines, (2) that the pragmatic argument is not one of James's major arguments in the early essays and, in fact, is not appealed to by him in these essays in any kind of systematic or near-systematic way, (3) that the "right to believe" and the "will to believe" doctrines do not need or involve the pragmatic argument, and (4) that James's statements on the nature of truth in "The Will to Believe" are actually inconsistent with his later-developed, pragmatic theory of truth.

The point to notice is that in neither the "will to believe" nor the "right to believe" doctrines does James argue that faith is justified by the positive value it accrues. In both doctrines, holding beliefs that are helpful and valuable may be justified, but it is not their positive value that justifies holding them; in the one case it is the fact that the belief is in a statement that can be verified by belief in it and in the other it is the fact that the belief is in a proposition that is an alternative of a genuine option. James does speak, in the context of both doctrines, of beliefs' satisfying passional needs, but in neither doctrine is a belief justified just because it satisfies passional needs.

As far as the pragmatic theory of truth is concerned, we should first note the historical point that James did not come explicitly to formulate the principle of pragmatism until 1898, in his essay "Philosophical Conceptions and Practical Results."[12] This was at least three years after "The Will to Believe" was first written. Moreover, in a 1907 letter to H. M. Kallen, James says that his "Will to Believe" argument

should not complicate the question of what we mean by truth. Truth is constituted by verification actual or possible, and beliefs, *however* reached, have to be verified before they can count as true. The question whether we have a right to believe anything before verification concerns not the constitution of truth, but the policy of belief. . . . In that case, why isn't it "true," if it *fits* the facts perfectly?[13]

This seems to me to be a statement of the correspondence theory of truth, and what James says here seems to dovetail entirely with the notion of truth he works with in "The Will to Believe." As we have seen, he argues in this essay that there is no infallible criterion of truth, no bell that rings whenever we have truth in our grasp, but he also refuses to deny the existence of (absolute) truths, and he argues for continuing to hope and search for them. What is it, then, according to James, for a hypothesis to be "true"? He answers as follows: "If the total drift of thinking continues to confirm it, that is what he [an empiricist, e.g., James] means by its being true."[14] This is not the pragmatic notion of truth.

It follows that no criticism either of what I am calling the pragmatic argument or of the pragmatic theory of truth will have any relevance to the "right to believe" doctrine. Matson's criticisms and those of others may or may not be sound criticisms, but they will have no bearing on the rightness of the Jamesian doctrines I am considering here.

The final criticism I shall discuss in this chapter has to do with the relationship of James's "right to believe" doctrine to Pascal's Wager; more specifically, it concerns the question of whether or not James is committed to the view that beliefs can be voluntarily adopted or rejected. The criticism I refer to can be stated quite simply: it is that we cannot voluntarily change our beliefs and that if James is urging us to do so as part of the "right to believe" doctrine, the doctrine is mistaken.[15]

Pascal, of course, does hold that beliefs can be changed voluntarily. (Let us accordingly call this view *Pascal's doctrine*.) This is why he makes his famous suggestion to anyone who wants to believe or who has been convinced by the Wager-argument that he ought to believe:[16]

Learn from those who have been bound like you, and who now stake all their possessions. . . . Follow the way by which they began; by acting as if they believed, taking the holy water, having masses said, etc. Even this will naturally make you believe.

Pascal, then, is arguing that a person who does not have re-

beliefs can come to have them (1) if he wants to
them, and (2) if he acts as if he has them. (We need
estigate the question whether or not Pascal's advice
d.)

James quotes Pascal with what seems to be a degree of ap-
proval in "The Will to Believe," but it is not clear to what
extent James accepts Pascal's doctrine. He says:[17]

> We feel that a faith in masses and holy water adopted will-
> fully after such a mechanical calculation would lack the
> inner soul of faith's reality; and if we were ourselves in
> the place of the Deity, we should probably take particular
> pleasure in cutting off believers of this pattern from their
> infinite reward. It is evident that unless there be some
> pre-existing tendency to believe in masses and holy water,
> the option offered to the will by Pascal is not a living op-
> tion. Certainly no Turk ever took masses and holy water
> on its account; and even to us Protestants these means of
> salvation seem such foregone impossibilities that Pascal's
> logic, invoked for them specifically, leaves us unmoved
> . . . . The talk of believing by our volition seems, then,
> from one point of view, simply silly. From another point
> of view it is worse than silly, it is vile.

Obviously, James is ambiguous on this point. On the one
hand he seems to insist that a person cannot voluntarily
adopt a belief unless there is some "preexisting tendency" in
him toward the belief (here Pascal's doctrine is "silly"), but
on the other hand he seems to allow for voluntarily adopted
beliefs while insisting that they will be mechanical and in-
sincere (here Pascal's doctrine is "vile").

In a later passage James seems to admit that Pascal's doctrine is sound, though his broad definition of the term *willing nature* makes us wonder if he is actually talking about
beliefs *voluntarily* changed:[18]

> It is only our already dead hypotheses that our willing
> nature is unable to bring to life again. But what has made
> them dead for us is for the most part a previous action of

our willing nature of an antagonistic kind. When I say "willing nature," I do not mean only such deliberate volitions as may have set up habits of belief that we cannot now escape from—I mean all such factors of belief as fear and hope, prejudice and passion, imitation and partisanship, the circumpresence of our caste and set.

It should also be noted that James does use language in "The Will to Believe" that makes it natural for us to interpret him as affirming Pascal's doctrine:[19]

our right to adopt a believing attitude in religious matters.

the lawfulness of voluntarily adopted faith.

The question of having moral beliefs at all or not having them is decided by our will.

I . . . cannot see my way to accepting the agnostic rules for truth-seeking, or willfully agree to keep my willing nature out of the game.

We have the right to believe at our own risk any hypothesis that is live enough to tempt our will.

But, on the other hand, we have the later testimony of James himself that he was not advocating Pascal's doctrine in "The Will to Believe." In fact, it was in part this issue that made James deeply regret that he had entitled his essay "The Will to Believe." This point comes out in several of James's letters:[20]

The "will to believe" . . . is essentially a will of complacence, assent, encouragement, towards a belief already there.

What I meant by the title was the state of mind of the man who finds an impulse in him toward a believing attitude, and who resolves not to quench it simply because doubts of its truth are possible.

Thus it is difficult to know how to interpret James at this point. Perhaps it would be helpful, though, to make a distinction between three different sorts of behavior: (1) confirming, maintaining, refusing to squelch a belief that we already hold; (2) encouraging, pushing, a belief that we do not actually hold but that we have a "preexisting tendency" to hold; and (3) trying to create a belief that we do not actually hold and that we have no preexisting tendency to hold.

As regards (1), this is what James claims the "will to believe" is all about in the first of his letters quoted above. If he is saying that this is all that the "right to believe" doctrine claims—that there are cases where we are justified in continuing to hold a belief that we already hold—then James is not necessarily committed to accepting Pascal's doctrine, for behavior (1) does not involve Pascal's doctrine. However, at times James also argues as if the "right to believe" doctrine applies to behavior (2) as well—see the second James letter quoted above. Behavior (2) would involve trying to encourage an impulse toward a belief, perhaps by trying to overcome doubts or by trying not to succumb to philosophical or scientific scruples. James is clearly committed to the view that his kind of effort can succeed, which means that he accepts a kind of weakened version of Pascal's doctrine, namely, that we can voluntarily adopt a belief that we do not already hold as long as we have a preexisting tendency to hold it. Behavior (3) involves the strong version of Pascal's doctrine, the version that Pascal himself accepts, that is, the claim that we can voluntarily adopt a belief we do not already hold apart from any preexisting tendency to hold it as long as we desire to hold it.

As we have seen, James argues against this view in "The Will to Believe." He seems to identify "having a preexisting tendency toward a belief" with the belief's being "live." Thus we can see that merely desiring to adopt a belief is not enough and does not in itself constitute a preexisting tendency, for, as we saw earlier, to claim that a hypothesis is live to a given person is to claim more than (though it also involves the claim) that he merely desires to accept it. We can conclude, then, that James rejects the strong version of Pascal's doctrine (behavior (3), but accepts the weaker version (behavior (2)). This means that James does allow for what might be called "voluntarily adopted belief" (in the weaker sense), and that if it can be shown that this is a false or incoherent notion, James's version of the "right to believe" doctrine can be criticized on these grounds. I say "James's version," because it remains to be seen whether or not the doctrine really needs this notion. I will take up this question later.

There is another relevant point about James and Pascal, a clear difference between them that ought not be overlooked. Pascal's Wager is essentially an evangelistic device: his argument is an attempt to convert people to religious faith. (James notices this: he says that in the Wager Pascal "tries to force us into Christianity."[21]) But James's "right to believe" doctrine should not be viewed in this way. He is not trying to convince us that we should believe: he is only trying to convince us (if the belief is an alternative of a genuine option) that we are epistemologically justified in believing *if belief is what we want*. His doctrine also justifies refusing to believe (say, in God), if *that* is what we want. What James is opposing in the "right to believe" doctrine is Clifford's insistence that suspension of judgment is *always* the *only* justified attitude in cases involving lack of adequate evidence.

NOTES

1. This criticism has been made by several philosophers. See Hick, *Faith and Knowledge,* p. 55, and *Philosophy of Religion* (Englewood Cliffs, N.J.:

Prentice-Hall, Inc., 1963), pp. 65–66; Miller, "James's Doctrine of 'The Right to Believe'," pp. 547–48; Wallace I. Matson, *The Existence of God* (Ithaca, N.Y.: Cornell University Press, 1965), p. 207; George Santayana, *Character and Opinion in the United States* (New York: Anchor Books, 1956), pp. 46–50.

2. TWTB, pp. 1–2; SR, pp. 90, 95.

3. Santayana, *Character and Opinion*, p. 47; cf. also the exchange of letters in Perry, *Thought and Character*, 2: 236–37.

4. Perry, *Thought and Character*, 2: 237. Cf. William MacLeod, "James's 'Will to Believe': Revisited," *The Personalist* 48 (1967): pp. 151–52.

5. *A History of Western Philosophy*, pp. 814–16.

6. Robert W. Beard, " 'The Will To Believe' Revisited," *Ratio* 8 (Dec. 1966) :174–76.

7. FATRTB, p. 228.

8. TWTB, pp. 2–3; p. 29 n. 1; ILWL. p. 54; SR, p. 90.

9. Matson, *Existence of God*, pp. 207–8, 213.

10. Ibid., 213–14.

11. ILWL, p. 52; italics added.

12. See William James, *Collected Essays and Reviews* (New York: Russell and Russell, 1920), pp. 411–12.

13. Perry, *Thought and Character*, 2: 249.

14. TWTB, p. 17.

15. See especially Miller, " 'The Will to Believe' and The Duty to Doubt," pp. 171, 183–85, 189; "James's Doctrine of 'The Right To Believe'," pp. 548–49, 555–58. In his first article Miller is not actually arguing against Pascal's doctrine; in fact, he agrees with it: "As we have seen, a belief may be produced by will" (p. 193 n). But in the second article he has clearly changed his mind: "A belief is not a voluntary conception; it is precisely an involuntary conception" (p. 548).

16. Pascal, *Pensées* (New York: E. P. Dutton and Company, Inc., 1958), p. 68.

17. TWTB, pp. 6–7. Cf. also pp. 4–8, 11, 21–22; SR, pp. 94–95 n.

18. TWTB, pp. 8–9.

19. TWTB, pp. 1, 2, 22–23, 18, 29.

20. Perry, *Thought and Character*, 2: 243, 244–45. Ducasse, however, accepts Pascal's doctrine. He argues for it and interprets James as accepting it. C. J. Ducasse, *A Philosophical Scrutiny of Religion* (New York: The Ronald Press Co., 1953), pp. 159–61, 165.

21. TWTB, p. 5.

8

Wishful Thinking

Let us define *wishful thinking* as believing a proposition to be true not because of evidence that it is true but because of a desire that it be true. Possibly the most substantive of the criticisms that have ever been made of the "right to believe" doctrine is the criticism that it opens the door to wishful thinking. Many critics have stressed that this is the most objectionable aspect of the doctrine, but probably the two most penetrating "wishful thinking" critics are Miller and Hick.

Miller originally made this criticism in his 1899 article, and his position never changed thereafter. He reaffirmed it in a 1927 review of Bixler's *Religion in the Philosophy of William James,* and again reaffirmed it in his 1942 article.[1] This last article is interesting because Miller wrote it fully conscious of the replies that James and his defenders had made to his earlier charges.[2] But Miller did not back down; he stuck to his guns and tried to justify his original criticisms.

Miller admits that very few propositions can actually be proved and that therefore we usually have to base our beliefs on low probability and even sometimes on a kind of educated intuition. But he strongly denies that this makes belief a matter of taste or that we can therefore believe propositions simply because we want to believe them. Desire is a poor guide to truth, Miller says. "Our wishes and goals are one thing; the stubborn necessities of the world in which we have to attain them by action are another." Wishful thinking is not only a fallacy, Miller says, but the source of all fallacy. It is actually a dangerous thing, first, because it is the foundation of such miseries as "war, destruction, torture, the ruin of lives, communities, civilizations," and second, because if practiced in one area, it will soon spread to others. Wishful thinking cannot be confined to one area alone. If we allow it to flourish, say, in religion, people will get in the habit of thinking wishfully, and soon it may spread to ethics, politics, or even science. James's "will to believe" is actually the will to deceive oneself, the will to hypnotize oneself into believing ill-founded propositions. "James took the worst weakness of the human mind, the bribery of the intelligence, and set it up as a kind of ideal. . . . The intervention of our 'passional nature,' of which James approves, is that which chiefly interferes, in all human beings, with good and trustworthy judgment."[3]

Hick claims that the "right to believe" doctrine "authorizes us to believe . . . any proposition, not demonstrably false, which it might be advantageous to us, in this world or another, to have accepted." He says that James tries to limit his doctrine to live options but, as we saw in chapter 6, Hick argues that the liveness of an option to us will be based on all kinds of accidental circumstances that have nothing whatsoever to do with the option's truth or falsity. Therefore it looks as if a person truly liberated from all such limiting circumstances would be free to embrace any possibly true option that he wanted to embrace. And since such a person would find that most of the religions of the world, for example, are mutually exclusive—in order to insure gaining one good he would have to risk losing another—his only rational course would be to embrace whatever religion offered him the greatest reward. And this, Hick says, gives an unrestricted license to wishful thinking. Thus, James's "right to believe" doctrine can be refuted by *reductio ad absurdum*, for it amounts to saying "that since the truth is unknown to us we may believe what we like and that while we are about it we had better believe what we like most."[4]

There are two possible routes a defender of James might take at this point. One way would be to meet the "wishful thinking" charge head-on by claiming that Miller and Hick have misrepresented James. This has been the usual approach that defenders of James have taken, and though I shall take a slightly different tack, I believe there is much to be said for this way of defending James. For the claim is that once one notices the strict limits James draws around his "right to believe" doctrine (i.e., the criteria of genuineness), there is no longer any ground for claiming that he is advocating wishful thinking. That is to say, only someone who has not paid close attention to the built-in limits of the doctrine could say that James is advocating "believing a proposition because you want to believe it."[5]

In support of this defense it could be pointed out that neither Miller nor Hick seems particularly careful in attending to the criteria of genuineness. As for Miller, he does not even mention the criteria in the 1899 article or in the 1927 review. He is finally aware of them in the 1942 article, but even here he only mentions them almost in passing. He seems to regard the liveness criterion (which we saw in chapter 6 is the most subjective of the four) as the crucial criterion, and he makes no effort to assess the "wishful thinking" charge in the light of the other three. The absence of any discussion of the ambiguity criterion is especially noticeable.

Hick is a more considered critic. He is careful to mention the four criteria in both his treatments of "The Will to Believe"; however, like Miller, he also seems to regard the liveness criterion as more important than the others, for in the context of his critical remarks about James this is the only criterion he mentions. And it is because Hick believes that this criterion (alone!) can be disposed of that he introduces the charge of wishful thinking, which he believes refutes the "right to believe" doctrine. So, like Miller, Hick does not bother to investigate the bearing that the other criteria have on this charge. This is perhaps why Hick feels it fair to summarize the "right to believe" doctrine as follows: "James is asserting . . . our right to believe at our own risk whatever we feel an inner need to believe."[6]

Thus it appears that a good case could be made that both "wishful thinking" critics have misrepresented the "right to believe" doctrine. Neither has paid close enough attention to the severe limits of the doctrine, and it appears that, once these limits are attended to, much of the force of their criticism is gone. James is definitely not asserting "our right to believe at our own risk whatever we feel an inner need to believe."

However, as I mentioned, my own attempt to answer the "wishful thinking" charge will be made on slightly different grounds. For despite the fact that Miller and Hick have not been entirely fair with James, I think a more careful "wishful thinking" critic could still claim that James is advocating wishful thinking. I do not say that he would be right, but I think that his criticism would be difficult to answer. For the more careful critic would not say that James is advocating "believing whatever proposition you want to believe" but rather "believing whatever proposition you want to believe that is an alternative of a genuine option." The latter formulation *is* fair to James's intentions in "The Will to Believe," and the critic could simply claim that it amounts to recommending wishful thinking.

We would then face the following question: Does "believing whatever proposition you want to believe that is an alternative of a genuine option" constitute wishful thinking or does it not? I think that this would be a difficult question to answer, and I suspect that debate on the question would end at an impasse: the critic claiming that it does and James's defender claiming that it does not. I do not see any immediate way that the dispute could be adjudicated. This is why I have decided to approach the wishful-thinking matter from a different angle. In part, my approach takes its cue from the impasse that I am supposing would obtain between the careful critic and the defender of James.

Let us return to the question Hick asks about James: "Is he not saying that since the truth is unknown to us we may believe what we like and that while we are about it we had better believe what we like most?" This does seem to put the "right to believe" doctrine in a bad light. Hick takes his question to be a refutation of James by *reductio ad absurdum*. He assumes that James is desperately trying to avoid the "wishful thinking" charge, but that it is the end result of the logic of his argument, and that therefore James is refuted once it is shown that he is, after all, advocating wishful thinking.

But I think that this is to misunderstand what James is really doing; it is to miss the subtlety of his argument. For I believe that James could defend himself in the following way (I do not claim that James would have defended himself in this way) : He could cheerfully admit that in a sense he is advocating wishful thinking, and then ask: "But what precisely is wrong with wishful thinking in evidence-situations involving genuine options?"

I suspect that if James were to make this move it would catch the critic off guard. For the critic has all along assumed without question that wishful thinking is something to be avoided: but now James asks the critic, "What is wrong with wishful thinking, that is, what is to prevent us from engaging in it?" Here the critic might appeal to the two fears expressed by Miller: that wishful thinking leads to all kinds of bad results and if allowed in one area will spread to others. But surely it is hard to see how bad results would follow from the kind of choice James is allowing, for he recommends choosing according to needs and hopes, that is, choosing what will lead to good results. And it is also hard to see how the kind of wishful thinking James is advocating could spread to other areas; surely the strict limits he sets for his doctrine would prevent this.

So if the critic were forced to think a bit more deeply on this question, I think that he could only conclude as follows: What normally prevents us from engaging in wishful thinking and what makes us think that wishful thinking is wrong is precisely Russell's Principle, which (he would say) we all accept as our criterion of rationality. For as we have seen, Clifford's version of the Principle says: "It is wrong always, everywhere, and for anyone, to believe anything on insufficient evidence." It is *this* that makes us feel that something is wrong in wishful thinking.

But here is where the subtlety of James's argument becomes clear. For it is not that James is stupidly flying in the face of Russell's Principle, as Miller and Hick seem to assume: it is that James is *questioning* the Principle, that is, he is denying that it always holds. For on James's view, the Principle is not universally applicable, as the critic has always assumed. There are cases where the Principle need not guide us. Moreover, the Principle itself, or at least the acceptance of it, is an expression of a personal epistemological attitude. James says: "The agnostic 'thou shalt not believe without coercive sensible evidence' is simply an expression (free to anyone to make) of private personal appetite for evidence of a peculiar kind."[7] So James is not so much *violating* Russell's Principle; he is *denying that it is always applicable*. And James's "right to believe" doctrine is an elaborate attempt to show us exactly where the Principle no longer holds, namely, in genuine options.

Thus James's "right to believe" doctrine turns out to be much more formidable than either Miller or Hick supposed. For in the light of James's attack on Russell's Principle, it will no longer cut any ice to "refute" James by arguing that he has advocated wishful thinking.

One possible way of testing the "right to believe" doctrine

would be to look at specific real or imagined cases of genuine options and see whether or not James's claim that we are free from Russell's Principle in such cases seems to be sound. One of the deficiencies of James's argument is that he fails to do so: he cites only broad, general themes, for example, what he calls "moral questions" or "the religious hypothesis." An examination of such cases might create a suspicion that he is right, or perhaps show us the reason his argument is wrong. But then again, it might just lead us into another impasse. Let us see.

At any rate, it seems to me that this is a strategy our "careful critic" might adopt against James. That is, he might quite simply try to come up with a counterexample to the "right to believe" doctrine. This counterexample would have to be a genuine option where Russell's Principle seems to hold. For since the nub of the "right to believe" doctrine is that the Principle does not hold in cases involving genuine options, the critic will have successfully refuted James if he can come up with even one such counterexample.

Let us imagine the following situation:[8] while entering a steep downgrade, a truck driver suddenly discovers that his brakes have failed. The truck begins to pick up speed and the driver sees that he will soon be in real danger. In this situation, the driver is faced with a choice: he can either jump from the truck, risking some bruises and broken bones while escaping the greater danger of a possible crash farther down the hill, or he can remain in the truck, risking a crash but hoping eventually to guide the truck down the hill to a level spot. But the driver does not know how far it is till the end of the grade, for this stretch of the road is new to him. At this point, we may conclude, the driver's option either to jump or to stay with the truck is a genuine option: live, because both alternatives appeal to him as distinct possibilities; forced, because he has no third choice; momentous, because his life is at stake; and the evidence is ambiguous, because to him neither possibility seems clearly safer than the other. Thus James would say that the will or passional nature of the driver may justifiably take over and do the deciding.

But here is where our careful critic would disagree and try to turn the truck-driver situation into a counterexample. For the critic would claim that the will and desires of the driver have nothing whatever to do with his making the right choice. If his will were to dictate, say, that he jump, this could by no stretch of the imagination guarantee that he would be justified in jumping; for it may be that he should instead have stayed in the truck. What the driver should do, the critic would assert, is to make his decision *on the basis of the available evidence.* Of course, the critic will have to admit that there is no evidence immediately available to the driver that will conclusively support one alternative over the other (this is why I said that the ambiguity criterion was satisfied here). But the critic can still claim that the driver has no other justifiable choice than to make up his mind on the basis of whatever evidence is available to him: his own driving abilities, the speed of the truck, the appearance of the road ahead, the terrain at the side of the road (where he could possibly jump), and so on.

In other words, the critic can claim that Russell's Principle still holds in cases such as this for the simple reason that the driver's passional nature might opt for the wrong alternative, the one that is actually more dangerous than the other. Thus James is wrong, he will say, in claiming that Russell's Principle does not hold in evidence-situations that are instances of genuine options. (One difficulty with this example is that the driver will have to weigh the evidence almost instantaneously, and James clearly had more reflective instances of genuine options in mind. But the critic can argue with perhaps some justification that this is irrelevant to his main point, that the driver is still obliged to base his decision on evidence alone, quick as his thinking would have to be.)

Here we find ourselves, at least initially, at the impasse I referred to earlier. For despite the critic's claim that the driver is not free to let his passional nature decide, James might simply insist that since his four criteria are satisfied, the driver *is* so free. That is, James might say to the critic: "Just *saying* that the driver must be guided by whatever evidence he can find, however meager it may be, does not *prove* that he must." But then, of course, the critic could reply in turn: "Just *saying* that the fulfillment of the four criteria frees the driver from Russell's Principle does not prove that it does."

I believe that the difficulty we face here arises from what I called in chapter 6 the "ambiguity problem." This is the problem of deciding how ambiguous the evidence must be in an evidence-situation (or in what way it has to be ambiguous) before the ambiguity criterion is satisfied. It will be recalled that in my discussion of this criterion I mentioned five different situations in which it might be claimed that the ambiguity criterion is satisfied for a given proposition p.

(8)   No evidence is now available or ever will be available relative to the truth or falsity of p.

(9)   No evidence is now available relative to the truth or falsity of p and there will probably never be any.

(10) No evidence is now available relative to the truth or falsity of p but at some time in the future evidence will probably be available.

(11) No sufficient, adequate, coercive evidence is now available relative to the truth or falsity of p. There is only a slight preponderance of evidence for p over not-p (or vice versa).

(12) The evidence for p and against not-p is evenly balanced with the evidence for not-p and against p, i.e., the evidence for p and against not-p is neither stronger nor weaker than the evidence for not-p and against p.

I concluded tentatively that the ambiguity criterion is satisfied wherever a rational person acting on the basis of the available evidence alone would be unable to make up his mind on the truth or falsity of p: the evidence must be ambiguous enough to fail to justify a choice. This seemed to include all five of the above evidence-situations. But does it?

I do not think that there can be much question about situations (8) and (12). It seems entirely clear that the "right to believe" doctrine is correct in such cases, and cannot be refuted by the "wishful thinking" charge. That is, in a situation where a decision must be made in a forced option between two alternatives and where evidence for and against each alternative is either absent altogether or evenly balanced, there the doctrine is sound. Frankly, I fail to see how any intelligent person could deny that in such cases a decision can justifiably be made on some basis other than the basis of evidence. My optimism may be unwarranted, but I think that anyone should be able to see that James is right here. For if we have to decide (forcedness criterion) and if we cannot decide on the basis of evidence (ambiguity criterion), it follows that we will have to decide on some basis other than evidence.

Admittedly, in most cases it would be quite difficult to say for sure that a given evidence-situation was an instance of situation (12), that is, a situation where the evidence for and against each alternative is exactly even. But we can imagine situations where this might be true. Take a situation where I need to know whether to turn right or left at the next intersection in order to reach my destination. Suppose that the only available evidence is one total stranger's recommendation that I turn right and another total stranger's recommendation that I turn left. This could be said to be a situation (12) kind of case, for the fact that the recommenders are strangers means that I do not know which is in a better position to know which way I should turn, which is a more trustworthy person, and so on.

Furthermore, I think that the "right to believe" doctrine is correct in situations (9) and (10) as well. For the only difference from (8) and (12) is that in (9) and (10) evidence *may* some day be available that will decide the issue. Thus the critic might conceivably recommend suspending judgment in such cases in the hope that conclusive evidence will one day be available. But of course this would be vain advice. For if the option is forced, a decision (pragmatically) *must* be made; and again, since the decision cannot be made on the basis of evidence, it can justifiably be made on some other basis—which is the heart of the "right to believe" doctrine.

Our difficulties, then, involve situation (11), cases where the available evidence favors one alternative over the other but only very slightly. And I think it is our difficulty with situation (11) that led to the impasse on the truck-driver case. Situations (8), (9), and (10) do not apply to the truck-driver case because the critic is right that there *is* evidence available: the speed of the truck, the lie of the land ahead, and so on. But it would be very surprising if the truck-driver case turned out to be a situation (12) type of case, that is, if it turned out that both options—jumping or staying in the truck—were exactly equal in objective danger.

The objective danger involved in each alternative could conceivably be determined by a team of scientists conducting experiments on the hill with similar trucks going the same speed and with volunteer drivers trying both alternatives. And as I say, it would be surprising if they did not conclude that one alternative was actually safer than the other. (The problem for the original driver, of course, was that in the midst of the situation he did not have all the evidence before him, and did not have time to weigh it all even if he did. He did not have the luxury of suspending judgment and waiting for the report of the scientists.)

Thus we can see that in all probability the truck-driver case fits in situation (11), though of course there is always the possibility that the report of the scientists would show that one alternative is considerably safer than the other. But, again, the question is : Can a situation (11) type of case ever satisfy the ambiguity criterion and, if so, how close does the evidence for and against the alternatives actually have to be before the criterion is satisfied? It will obviously have to be quite close, for Miller is right that there are few propositions that we can actually prove, and so most decisions between two alternatives have to be made on the basis of probability. In many cases, of course, the probability is so high for one alternative and so low for the other that we have no problem deciding. But we also often have to make decisions on the basis of a very small difference in probability between the two alternatives. It would appear, then, that if the ambiguity criterion is to be satisfied, the probabilities for each alternative will have to be so close that a rational person in a normal situation could not make a decision on the basis of the evidence alone.

The thing to notice, however, is that when the careful critic claims that the driver should make up his mind on the basis of whatever evidence is available to him, in so doing he rules that this is a case that *can* be decided on the basis of evidence, which means that the ambiguity criterion is not satisfied and that the truck-driver case is not a genuine counterexample to the "right to believe" doctrine. Thus James might say to the critic: "Of course: if this is a case that can be decided on the basis of evidence, the option is not genuine and the 'right to believe' doctrine does not apply." Here, then, is the crucial question: Can (should) the truck-driver case be decided on the basis of evidence or can (should) it not? What is our criterion for distinguishing between situation (11) type of cases that can be decided by evidence and those that cannot?

There is a possible criterion that has some promise of moving us beyond our impasse, and I have alluded to it already. Let us say that a situation (11) type of case can be decided on the basis of evidence when there is enough of a preponderance of evidence for one alternative over the other to justify a rational person in a normal situation in making a choice on the basis of evidence. This criterion puts the ball back into the critic's court; in effect it says, "You be the one to decide; the ambiguity criterion is satisfied whenever you, the critic, in a normal situation would rule (1) that the preponderance of evidence for one alternative over the other is insufficient to justify a rational choice, and (2) that the wisest choice is therefore suspension of judgment."

However, this criterion will have to be refined slightly. For the critic could make the following reply: "But when you speak of a 'normal case' you can only be talking about a nonforced option where we have the luxury of suspending judgment and wait for further evidence. But in the case of a forced option where, by your own rules, whatever we do, a decision will be made, our standards of evidence obviously cannot be quite so high. Thus our rule in cases of forced options would be: 'Always decide on the basis of whatever relevant evidence you have.' Even if there is only a very slight preponderance of evidence for one alternative over the other, always choose the alternative that is favored by the available evidence."

I think that James is right that it is the critic's fear of being in error that motivates him in disputes such as this.[9] This can be seen from the critic's response to the truck-driver case: his objection to allowing the driver to decide on the basis of his passions rather than on the basis of what meager evidence he has is the familiar one that his passions may dictate his making what will turn out to be the wrong choice.

Perhaps now the criterion we need is in sight. Let us say that the will or the passions can justifiably determine choice in a situation (11) kind of forced option where the preponderance of evidence in favor of one alternative over the other is so slight that choosing on the basis of evidence gives no better chance of making what will turn out to be the correct choice than choosing on the basis of the will or the passions. It will probably be difficult to say precisely when this criterion is satisfied and when it is not. But nevertheless I think most people have a sophisticated enough "feel" for evidence to be able to determine with a good degree of reliability when the available evidence is so meager as to be unhelpful.

Let us return to the decision I face whether to turn right

or left. To change the example slightly, suppose that the only evidence I have is gained in this way: A man is driving the opposite way from the way that I am going; he stops, and I ask him which way to turn; he shouts something at me and then drives on; I feel sure that he shouted "Turn left!" but my wife, who is with me, insists that he shouted "Turn right!"; the man's shout is the *only* evidence we have; what do we do? This seems to be a situation (12) type of case, but it actually belongs in situation (11). Why? Because I was sitting in the driver's seat and was therefore two feet closer than my wife to the man who shouted the instructions. Thus, possibly, I was in a better position to hear what he said.

I do not know whether our new criterion would be satisfied in this case or not. It seems to me that it would be, but the critic could always deny it. But the point is, *if* this is a case where acting on the basis of the *very slight* preponderance of evidence that we have discovered for one alternative over the other promises us no better chance of making the right decision than acting on the basis of the will or the passions, then the ambiguity criterion is satisfied and the "right to believe" doctrine will apply.

The critic is supposing that the rule "In situation (11) type of cases always act on the basis of whatever evidence you have" will in the long run lead to fewer errors than the rule "In situation (11) type of cases you may justifiably act on the basis of the will." This may or may not be true, and it would obviously be very difficult to prove or disprove. What I am claiming, however, is that there are situation (11) type of cases where the preponderance of evidence in favor of one alternative over the other is so slight that we have no way of telling which method of deciding will lead to fewer errors. In such cases, I claim, the ambiguity criterion is satisfied and, if the option is also forced, James's "right to believe" doctrine can be invoked.

We may conclude, then, that the "right to believe" doctrine cannot be refuted by means of the wishful-thinking criticism. My own view is that the pragmatic argument is open to this

charge, but since the "right to believe" doctrine does not depend on the pragmatic argument, this will have no bearing on
the present issue. James may or may not be advocating wishful
thinking; this depends on whether or not we choose to call
"believing whatever proposition you want to believe that
is an alternative of a genuine option" wishful thinking. If
we do not, then James is immune to the charge. If we do,
James can then ask: "All right, but what exactly is wrong with
wishful thinking in cases involving genuine options?" We
have seen that none of the answers the critic makes to this
question are acceptable, at least as regards evidence-situations
(8) through (12). This means that the "right to believe"
doctrine cannot be refuted by means of the wishful-thinking
charge.

I now wish to look briefly at James's "will to believe" doctrine, the doctrine that faith is sometimes self-verifying, the
doctrine that a willingness to act as if p were true can at
times make p true. We need to ask several questions here:
(1) What precisely does the doctrine mean?; (2) Is the doctrine acceptable?; and (3) how does the doctrine relate (if
it does relate) to the "right to believe" doctrine?

This doctrine was obviously one of James's pet theories:
he pushes it in several of his early essays as well as in some
of his later works. He gives many illustrations of situations
in which faith can be self-verifying. If I believe that life is
worth living, this belief can bring it about that life will be
meaningful to me. If I believe that I am going to gain a promotion on the job, this belief can bring it about that I will
gain a promotion. If I believe that a given person likes me,
this belief can bring it about that he will like me. If the
various members of an athletic team believe that each team-
mate is going to do his job to the best of his ability, this belief can bring it about that the players will perform to the
best of their ability.[10]

However, James's most vivid illustration of the "will to
believe" (which unfortunately he did not include in "The

Will to Believe") is that of a mountain climber in the Alps who finds himself in a spot where only a fairly long leap across a chasm will save him.[11]

> In this case . . . the part of wisdom clearly is to believe what one desires; for belief is one of the indispensable pre-liminary conditions of the realization of its object. *There are then cases where faith creates its own verification.* Believe, and you shall be right, for you shall save yourself; doubt, and you shall again be right, for you shall perish. The only difference is that to believe is greatly to your advantage.

> In such a case (and it belongs to an enormous class), the part of wisdom as well as courage is to *believe what is in the line of your needs,* for only by such belief is the need fulfilled.

In cases where belief creates its own verification, then, we are not only justified in believing more than the evidence strictly warrants, but we must believe. For belief is one of the conditions of verification.

Let us call a "W-statement" any proposition to which the "will to believe" doctrine applies. James appears to be making two claims about W-statements: (1) that they can be verified by means of faith in their truth, and (2) that they can *only* be verified by means of faith in their truth. It would appear, then, that there are three criteria that a proposition must satisfy before it can be considered a W-statement, the first two of which must be satisfied for a W-statement that can be verified by means of faith in its truth (and can perhaps also be verified by other means as well), and all three of which must be satisfied for a W-statement that can be verified *only* by means of faith in its truth.

(1) The truth of the proposition has yet to be determined, i.e., it is a proposition about future facts.

(2) My faith in the proposition can verify the proposition.

(3)   The proposition can be verified *only* if I have faith in it.

It is unclear whether or not James would want to make a distinction between the set of W-statements that can be verified by means of faith and the set of W-statements that can be verified *only* by means of faith. Perhaps he would do so, but perhaps, on the other hand, he would want to claim that only those propositions which can be verified only by means of faith are W-statements. At times he does seem to indicate the latter,[12] but some of his examples clearly imply the former. Surely my belief that Jones likes me is not the *only* way the proposition "Jones likes me" can be verified.

But there is also another unclarity in the "will to believe" doctrine as well. Is James saying that in the case of W-statements my prior faith in their truth is actually what brings about their later verification, or is he merely saying that my prior faith *helps* bring about their later verification? Is he saying that faith can be a sufficient condition of verification or only a necessary condition? The former might be called the "strong version" of the "will to believe" doctrine and the latter the "weak version." Unfortunately, there is textual evidence for both versions in each of the three early essays.

For example, the strong version seems to be implied in such statements as:[13]

There are then cases where faith creates its own verification.

The desire for a certain kind of truth here brings about that special truth's existence. . . . Faith . . . creates its own verification.

Often enough our faith beforehand in an uncertified result *is the only thing that makes the result come true.*

The weak version is implied in such statements as:[14]

There is a certain class of truths of whose reality belief is a factor as well as a confessor.

There are, then, cases where a fact cannot come at all unless a preliminary faith exists in its coming. And when faith in a fact can help create the fact, that would be an insane logic which . . .

These, then, are my last words to you: Be not afraid of life. Believe that life *is* worth living, and your belief will help create the fact.

Both the confusion about the strong and the weak version of the "will to believe" doctrine and about the presence or absence of the third criterion of W-statements illustrate James's all-too-frequent failure to make his meaning clear and his regrettable failure to think through the implications of the distinctions he makes. However, I do not think that either problem requires further serious consideration for present purposes. Let us simply accept the weaker version of the doctrine and the third criterion. Thus a W-statement will be any proposition that satisfies all three criteria, where criterion (2) is changed slightly to read, "My faith in the proposition can *help* verify the proposition." I make this last suggestion because aside from textual evidence about what James must have meant, it would be odd to claim that a given proposition can be verified by my faith *alone*. Surely other factors would enter in as well: to take the mountain climber case, surely the strength of his legs, the weight of his clothing and equipment, how fatigued he is, and the like would also be involved in verifying the possible W-statement "I can leap across this chasm."

In this way we can also answer an objection that Kaufmann raises.[15]

It is not even true, though James shared this belief with

most Americans of his time and of our own, that to succeed one must believe one will succeed. If you should try to jump across a ditch which all but passes your capacity, what is decisive is not that you believe you will succeed but that you should give it all you have. If you have faith but do not try as hard as possible, you will not succeed. If you should think that it is most unlikely that you will succeed, but nevertheless you try as hard as you can, you may succeed. What matters is not faith but effort; and that effort without faith that we shall succeed is either psychologically impossible or doomed to failure, while faith spells success, that is a myth which most Americans believe—without sufficient evidence.

Since we have now rejected the strong version of the "will to believe" doctrine, we can answer Kaufmann's objection by restating James's argument slightly. Let us now say that the "will to believe" doctrine claims that there are cases where if you both try as hard as you can and believe that you will succeed you are more likely to succeed than if you try as hard as you can but doubt that you will succeed, and that there are cases where if you try as hard as you can you will succeed *only* if you also believe that you will succeed. In this way, James is not put in the position of denying that effort is important. Kaufmann might be correct (1) that effort without faith is psychologically possible, (2) that there are cases where we can have faith and fail because of lack of effort, and (3) that there are cases where we can succeed apart from faith because of effort; but these facts will not affect the amended "will to believe" doctrine.

The "will to believe" is clearly connected with James's belief in what he calls a "melioristic universe." We need not dwell on this point, but James clearly needs to posit an open-ended kind of universe if the "will to believe" is to be at all plausible. That is, he needs what he calls an unfinished world, a world that can be affected and altered by our actions.

In a determined, closed, set world, my faith in my ability to leap across a chasm will presumably have no effect on the state of the world, that is, on my ability to succeed in my attempt. But in a melioristic, pluralistic, cooperative universe, my faith, my hope, my freedom can have a profound effect on the future state of the universe. Indeed, says James, in such a universe we can help create the kind of world we are looking for. Thus "Faith. . . . may be regarded as a formative factor in the universe, if we be integral parts thereof, and co-determinants, by our behavior, of what its total character may be." "The melioristic universe . . . will succeed just in proportion as more people work for its success. If none work, it will fail. If each does his best, it will not fail."[16]

The obvious question we should raise here is, How much of the universe is melioristic? Surely some facts cannot be affected by my faith—the distance between two galaxies, for instance—but if the "will to believe" doctrine is sound, some facts can be affected by my faith. But where are we to draw the line? That is, what are the limits of the "will to believe"? We shall return to this question later, but first we should ask the question that is logically prior: Is James's doctrine correct at all? Can faith *ever* affect fact?

This looks to be a straightforward factual question rather than a philosophical question, but unfortunately I know of no work in psychology or any other discipline that would confirm or disconfirm James's doctrine. Some views close to James's were held by Joseph Jastrow, a psychologist and contemporary of James. Jastrow tells us (1) that a student's belief about how difficult an upcoming examination will be can actually affect his performance. "When one has once formed the impression, or has had it produced or suggested for him, that the study or task he is about to attack is a difficult one, his mental powers are at once sufficiently reduced to make it really difficult." He also reports (2) that "in jumping or running and in other athletic trials, the entertainment of a notion of a possible failure to reach the mark lessens the intensity of one's effort, and prevents the accomplishment of one's best."[17] However, Jastrow's illustrations are far too anecdotal in nature to be accepted uncritically. Unfortunately he does not verify them with experimental data.

Perhaps we had better leave the matter open. I must confess I tend to believe that James is right. It seems to me that there are situations where faith is self-verifying,[18] and this is a doctrine that seems to be popularly held (under such rubrics as "the power of positive thinking"), but I do not know whether or not anyone has tested the doctrine nor, frankly, do I see how it could be tested.

Aside from the question of experimental confirmation, the "will to believe" doctrine has been subjected to philosophical criticism as well. The most serious is the point I raised earlier: If we grant that the doctrine is sound, what are its limits? Where does it apply and where does it not apply?

For it is obvious (as I mentioned earlier) that there are certain facts that no faith could conceivably even help to bring about. If faith can create facts, then, it must be only a certain range or type of fact. But what range or type? Unfortunately, James does not tell us. However, I do not think it is true to claim that James does not realize the obvious fact that the "will to believe" applies only to some kinds of facts and not to others. For James admits that

> the future movements of the stars or the facts of past history are determined now once for all, whether I like them or not. They are given irrespective of my wishes, and in all that concerns truths like these subjective preference should have no part; it can only obscure the judgment.

And he goes on to say that the range of facts to which the "will to believe" applies is "every fact into which there enters an element of personal contribution on my part."[19] Thus it would seem that, if sound at all, the doctrine will apply to those facts or potential facts whose existence depends wholly or in part on circumstances that are under my control or that I can affect by my actions. Therefore James knows that his doctrine has limits.

However, James *can* be charged with failure to specify carefully these limits. That is, he knows that there are limits, but he does not tell us what they are; that is, he does not tell us which facts my "personal contribution" can affect and which it cannot. For example, it is obvious that no amount of faith could help the mountain climber leap across a forty-foot chasm. A defender of James might claim that he is talking about a much shorter chasm, and this would probably be so. But James should have said so, and his failure to say so gives at the very least the wrong impression.

Part of the reason that James's failure to do so is an important omission is the fact that in "The Will to Believe" he is trying to defend religious faith. Thus the obvious inference for the reader to draw is that the "will to believe" doctrine has some bearing on religious propositions; otherwise, why did James introduce the doctrine at all? But surely it would be strange to claim that faith can be self-verifying in matters of religion. How could my faith in God create God, or how could my faith in immortality create immortality? It may be that faith is necessary if we are to find God, or it may be that faith is necessary for obtaining further evidence that God exists. But these are different matters altogether. The question remains: How can the "will to believe" have any direct relevance to the question of the validity of religious faith?

James does drop some unformulated and vague hints in "Is Life Worth Living?" that the "will to believe" doctrine has religious or metaphysical implications.[20]

Is it not sheer dogmatic folly to say that our inner interests can have no real connection with the forces that the hidden world may contain?

But will our faith in the unseen world similarly verify itself? Who knows? . . . Once more it is a case of *maybe;* and once more *maybes* are the essence of the situation. I confess that I do not see why the very existence of an invisible world may not in part depend on the personal response which any one of us may make to the religious appeal. God himself, in short, may draw vital strength and increase of very being from our fidelity.

These thoughts, no doubt, are connected with James's "melioristic universe," but they are more puzzling than illuminating. In the first place, it is true that the term *God* might be taken to mean a kind of psychological construct in the believer's mind whereby "I believe in God" logically implies "God exists (for me)." In this sense, God's existence would indeed depend on my belief in him. But I see no evidence whatsoever that James is talking about this kind of God. It is clear that in his essays he is talking about a God who is a real being who exists independently of our belief in him, a God upon whom we depend for our existence rather than vice versa. Otherwise, why would James have felt the need to write "The Will to Believe?" For in the case of the psychological God, since my faith in him creates him (in me, so to speak), there is no need to defend the propriety of religious faith.

Hence it would seem that James's hints that the "will to believe" doctrine applies to God are too undeveloped and hazy to be of any help at all. James does not tell us *how* the existence of the "invisible world" can depend upon our belief or disbelief in it or how our fidelity can increase God's being. And it might be added as well that James does not explain the meaning of the qualifying phrase *in part* in the second passage quoted above.

Presently I will turn to the question of the relationship between the "will to believe" and the "right to believe" doctrines in James's early essays, but for now I wish simply to note that the "will to believe" does not seem to have any obvious application to such religious propositions as "God exists" or "The soul is immortal." The "will to believe" does have a certain role to play in religious faith, which I will discuss in chapter 9, but not this kind of role. Faith might help me win a contest or make a friend or overcome a temptation or even recover from an illness or make life worth living. But it certainly cannot create God.

To return for a moment to the dilemma of the truck driver discussed earlier in this chapter, we should note that James might appeal to the "will to believe" doctrine in relation to this case. But I think this appeal would turn out to have only limited relevance. James might conceivably argue that the driver can justifiably choose as his will directs, for if the driver believes that jumping from the truck will be the best policy, *it will be.* That is, he will be much more likely to jump safely if he believes that jumping is the better alternative than if he doubts it. Likewise, if he believes that staying in the truck will be the best policy, it will be, for the same reasons.

Now if the "will to believe" doctrine is ever correct, James is probably right that, whatever choice the driver makes, his performance will be helped if he firmly believes that he is making the right choice. But I think the claim that the driver can justifiably choose on the basis of his passions will be sound only in certain cases and not in others. For if one of the choices is in the long run actually safer than the other (as determined by the scientists), the driver would obviously be far better off to make the right choice, though he doubts that it is the right choice, than to make the wrong choice, though he firmly believes that it is the right choice. The critic would surely be right in saying here that the driver's passional nature may well opt for the wrong alternative. However, there is one case where James's argument will be quite sound. This is the case where there is no possibility of "opting for the wrong alternative," namely, a situation (12) type of case, a case where the two alternatives are exactly equal in objective danger.

Thus it seems that the "will to believe" doctrine will help James in the truck-driver case only if the two alternatives are equally dangerous. It will not help him if the problem is simply that it cannot immediately be determined which is more dangerous. But since I already noted that it would be surprising if the two alternatives turned out to be exactly equal in objective danger, this means that it would be surprising if the "will to believe" doctrine turned out to be applicable to the truck-driver case.

It is true that the "will to believe" is a separate doctrine from the "right to believe." (1) The "will to believe" is essentially a factual claim that in certain cases faith can be self-verifying, while the "right to believe" is an epistemological attempt to justify belief in nonevident propositions in certain cases. (2) The "will to believe" has no obvious application to such religious propositions as "God exists" or "The soul is immortal," while the "right to believe" clearly does. (3) Neither doctrine seems logically dependent on the other: each could be true even if the other is false. (4) In a case where the "will to believe" is correctly invoked, that is, where faith does verify itself, the "right to believe" doctrine cannot be invoked. For the ambiguity criterion of the "right to believe" doctrine rules out verification or conclusive evidence of any kind, whether brought about by faith or not.

I agree, then, that the two doctrines are separate, and I think that the "right to believe" is the essential and philosophically more important point in James's essay. However, there are some points of connection between the two doctrines, and I do not agree with Hick that the "will to believe" can be used only as a kind of psychological preparation for the "right to believe."[21] The connection is that both doctrines, in their own way, have to do with belief-policy, that is, with questions about when a person is epistemologically justified in believing a given proposition. Both attempt to justify belief in propositions that (1) are in line with our desires and hopes and (2) are nonevident. The one does so by means of the criteria of genuineness and the other does so by arguing that a proposition can be believed if believing it will verify it.

Thus, both the "right to believe" and the "will to believe" can be taken as saying, "You have the epistemological right to believe proposition p," where p is a certain carefully specified proposition. On the "right to believe" p must be a proposition that is an alternative of a genuine option and on the "will to believe" p must be a W-statement.[22]

NOTES

1. See Dickenson Miller, " 'The Will To Believe' and the Duty to Doubt," pp. 172–73, 187–88; review of Bixler's *Religion in the Philosophy of William James, Journal of Philosophy* 24 (1927) :209–10; "James's Doctrine of 'The Right To Believe,' " pp. 552–58.

2. See Perry, *Thought and Character,* 2:241, 245–48.

3. Miller, "James's Doctrine of 'The Right To Believe,' " pp. 552–54.

4. Hick, *Faith and Knowledge,* pp. 42, 44; cf. also his *Philosophy of Religion,* p. 66.

5. This is the line James himself took in defense of "The Will to Believe." In a letter to L. T. Hobhouse he writes: "My essay hedged the license to indulge in private over-beliefs with so many restrictions and signboards of danger that the outlet was narrow enough." Perry, *Thought and Character,* 2:245.

6. Hick, *Faith and Knowledge,* p. 40; see also p. 39 and *Philosophy of Religion,* pp. 65, 66. Hick is strongly criticized by MacLeod for failing to consider the momentousness and forcedness criteria. MacLeod, pp. 156–57.

7. ILWL, p. 56.

8. This illustration of a genuine option is close to an illustration used by Ducasse, *A Philosophical Scrutiny,* p. 164. See also P. Hare and E. Madden, "William James, Dickinson Miller, and C. J. Ducasse on the Ethics of Belief," *Transactions of the Charles Peirce Society* 4 (Fall 1968) :117. The truck-driver case occurred to me before I read Ducasse, which I point out only because the fact that two different philosophers would independently come up with virtually the same case as an instance of an option that satisfies all four criteria is perhaps a clue that there are not very many truly genuine options.

9. TWTB, pp. 17–19.

10. ILWL, pp. 59–62; TWTB, pp. 23–25; SR, pp. 91, 96–100, 105–9.

11. SR, p. 97; ILWL, p. 59; cf. SR, pp. 96–109.

12. ILWL, p. 59.

13. SR, p. 97; TWTB, p. 24; ILWL, p. 59.

14. SR, p. 96; TWTB, p. 25; ILWL, p. 62; cf. also SR, p. 91: ". . . as if he were individually helping to create the actuality of the truth whose metaphysical reality he is willing to assume."

15. Walter Kaufmann, *Critique of Religion and Philosophy* (Garden City, N.Y.: Doubleday and Company, 1961). p. 117.

16. FATRTB, pp. 225, 229.

17. Joseph Jastrow, *Fact and Fable in Psychology* (Boston: Houghton Mifflin Company, 1900), pp. 298, 301.

18. See Mark 11:20–23; Luke 17:6.

19. SR, p. 97. In TWTB James makes the same point by limiting the "will to believe" doctrine to "truths dependent on our personal action." See p. 25.

20. ILWL, pp. 55, 61.

21. Hick, *Faith and Knowledge,* p. 39.

22. Cf. TWTB, p. 25; SR, pp. 96, 97.

9

The Religious Hypothesis

There are two major tasks to complete in this chapter. It will have been noticed that I have made several modifications in the "right to believe" doctrine as I have proceeded—changes that I hope catch the spirit of what James was trying to say in "The Will to Believe" and that I believe will result in a more acceptable version of the doctrine. My first task, then, is to state as clearly as possible the version of the doctrine that I am defending, and show how it differs from (and, I hope, improves upon) James's own version in "The Will to Believe." The second task is to ask whether or not the amended doctrine has any application, whether or not there are any propositions to which the doctrine will apply and which can therefore be accepted on some basis other than evidence. Here I shall have to look at the main example James gives us of a "genuine option," namely, what he calls "the religious hypothesis." I will try to discover whether or not the "right to believe" doctrine can be applied to religious propositions, since this is the main point that James's essay was meant to establish.

The reader will have noticed that in chapter 8, where I attempted to defend the "right to believe" doctrine against the "wishful thinking" criticism, I concentrated almost entirely on the forcedness and ambiguity criteria. This reflects the conclusion I reached at the end of chapter 6 that these two criteria are really all that James needs to make his doctrine work. I called a situation in which the forcedness and ambiguity criteria are satisfied a *Jamesian case.*

The reason I believe that a Jamesian case is all that is required is as follows. It seems to me that the advice of the Intellectualist really amounts to this: "Choose between any two alternative hypotheses only on the basis of evidence, and where a choice on such a basis cannot be made, make no choice at all, that is, suspend judgment." We can see, then, that the two criteria are all that James really needs, for the ambiguity criterion rules out choosing on the basis of evidence and the forcedness criterion rules out not choosing. This means (1) that a choice must be made and (2) that the choice must be made on some basis other than the available evidence. And this is precisely James's "right to believe" doctrine.

James puts it slightly differently; he says that where the "right to believe" doctrine applies, we can decide between the two alternatives *on the basis of our passional nature.* This apparently means that our will or "volitional nature" can do the deciding, and that the decision can justifiably be made on the basis of our hopes or emotions or desires. This is not exactly what I am saying—that where the doctrine applies we can choose *on some basis other than evidence*—but perhaps the two formulations are not too different. For in the discussion of James's use of the term *passional nature* in chapter 5, we saw that this term is mainly meant to exclude the intellectual nature, which, among other things, is the faculty for making decisions on the basis of evidence. In other words, I am claiming that all that the "right to believe" doctrine actually justifies is a choice that can be made on some basis other than evidence. But if it could be shown that there are only two possible bases on which choice can ever be made—intellect and passion—then James's formulation does not really differ from mine.

But perhaps this is not too serious a problem anyway. Even

if there turn out to be *many* possible bases on which decisions can be made—say, intellect, passion, expediency, flipping a coin (assuming that the last three are really different bases), this will not matter. For the "right to believe" doctrine does not say on which nonevidential basis choice can justifiably be made, but just that it can justifiably be made on a non-evidential basis. Presumably, then, *any* nonevidential basis will do, even flipping a coin. (Perhaps flipping a coin would be excluded by the requirements of the "will to believe" doctrine or for other reasons, however.)

Let me now state the "right to believe" doctrine that I have arrived at and believe to be sound.

Where a person is faced with a forced option between two mutually exclusive hypotheses and where a decision between the two hypotheses cannot be made on the basis of evidence, with full epistemological justification he can choose between the hypotheses on some basis other than evidence and can tentatively (i.e., with his mind still open) accept the hypothesis chosen and act as if it were true.

Before considering the ways in which this amended "right to believe" doctrine differs from James's original version, two points ought to be noticed. The first is that both versions of the doctrine are open to an interpretation that I have not emphasized. Not only would it be true to say that in a genuine option a person "can justifiably choose" on some basis other than evidence; it would also be true to say that he "must" do so, he has no other choice, this is all he can do.[1] Choice on some other basis, then, is not only justifiable but unavoidable. Even a decision to suspend judgment, which (as we have seen) in effect amounts to accepting one of the alternatives, will be a passional decision. And if such a decision is unavoidable, it must, because it is unavoidable, also be epistemologically justifiable: or at least the question of whether or not it is epistemologically justifiable need not even be raised. For if a given decision is inevitable, it is pointless to worry about whether or not it is justifiable.

The second point, as stated in the amended version, is that the doctrine will allow only *tentative* acceptance of the hypothesis chosen. James stresses that we keep an open mind for future evidence, and this attitude seems to be required by the doctrine. There could theoretically be cases where the conclusion need not be accepted tentatively: situations where it is known in advance that there will never be additional evidence available that is relevant to the truth value of the alternatives. But it is difficult to imagine an option about which it could be known in advance that the evidence will be permanently ambiguous. If there are such cases, they are obviously rare.

So it follows that in the vast majority of the cases to which the "right to believe" doctrine applies, if not in all of them, the conclusion can be accepted only tentatively. By *tentatively,* however, I do not necessarily mean "weakly." The conclusion can be accepted firmly, I would think, as long as it is not accepted in such a way as to close the believer's mind to future evidence. This point undoubtedly raises some questions about the relevance of the "right to believe" doctrine to religious faith. For some would claim that it would be false to say of the typical religious believer that the religious propositions he accepts on faith—for example, that God exists, that Christ rose from the dead on the third day—are accepted tentatively. I will return to this point in chapter 10.

Let me now mention six important ways in which the amended version of the "right to believe" doctrine differs from, and, I hope, improves upon, the original version.

(1)   The amended version is carefully distinguished from the "will to believe" doctrine. while the original was not.

(2)   The amended version is not based on acceptance of James's dictum that "there is no test of the truth." James apparently thinks that his version depends on this dictum and Miller interprets James in this way, but I have argued that the doctrine does not require this assumption. It should be

added, however, that the amended version does not depend on a rejection of the dictum either.

(3) The amended version makes use of only the forcedness and ambiguity criteria, while the original version requires the liveness and momentousness criteria as well. This reduces the doctrine to its essentials and eliminates the need to salvage two criteria that raise serious difficulties for the defender of James.

(4) The amended version does not require the view that belief equals tendency to act. The phrase *and act as if it were true* in the amended version is not necessarily meant to imply or be implied by *can tentatively accept the hypothesis*. So it will not matter whether James or Matson is correct on this question. (The elimination of the momentousness and liveness criteria helps here as well, for I think it was mainly in the context of discussion of these criteria that James needed the doctrine that belief equals tendency to act.)

(5) The amended version does not involve any commitment one way or the other on the matter of whether or not beliefs can be voluntarily adopted. Simply saying that in a certain kind of situation we have the epistemological right to hold a certain kind of belief, as the amended doctrine does, says nothing about whether or not such a belief is being held by a given person, can be created by him, can be created if he has a preexisting tendency to believe it, et cetera. The amended "right to believe" doctrine could still be true even if it turns out that *no* version of Pascal's doctrine is sound.

(6) The amended version has no need and makes no use of any arguments about whether or not the "believe truth" rule takes priority over the "avoid error" rule.

Opinion has differed widely on the extent of the range of propositions to which the "right to believe" doctrine can be applied. Miller and Hick, the "wishful thinking" critics, argue that the doctrine applies to an enormous class of propositions, and thus encourage too much license in belief.[2] But Beard argues that the doctrine imposes such severe restrictions as to be relatively innocuous: it can be doubted, he says, whether even moral or religious propositions can pass all the tests.[3] (It should be noted that Beard's view undoubtedly follows from his rather strict version of the notion of a genuine option. But since I am claiming that the "right to believe" doctrine needs only the two criteria of a Jamesian case, it seems probable to me that there are some propositions that satisfy the requirements of the doctrine, and thus that the doctrine is not innocuous.)

In section 9 of "The Will to Believe," where we are led to expect and hope that James will begin giving us examples of genuine options, he only mentions such broad categories as *moral questions* and *questions concerning personal relations.* He stresses that in the case of options that belong in these categories we cannot wait for conclusive evidence and that the passions and the will are at work in creating our convictions. But the problem is that he then attempts to show not that these options are genuine but that they are W-statements, that is, propositions to which the "will to believe" doctrine will apply. This is one of the points where one feels it a shame that James apparently failed to see the distinction between his two doctrines.

James next turns to what he calls "the religious hypothesis," which fortunately he does try to show is genuine. He gives us a concise formulation of this hypothesis. Religion, he claims, says essentially two things:[4]

First, she says that the best things are the more eternal things, the overlapping things, the things in the universe that throw the last stone, so to speak, and say the final word. "Perfection is eternal,"—this phrase of Charles Secretan seems a good way of putting this first affirmation of religion, an affirmation which obviously cannot yet be verified scientifically at all.

The second affirmation of religion is that we are better

off even now if we believe her first affirmation to be true.

Our first reaction might be to wonder what "the religious hypothesis" has to do with the actual religions of the world. Surely no religion says precisely this. James explains, however, that the religions differ so in their "accidents" (by which he perhaps means their particular dogmas, institutions, and rituals) that discussion of each is precluded. What is needed is a generic, inclusive description of (the essence of?) religion, and this is what his "religious hypothesis" was meant to provide. (Whether or not it does provide an accurate distillation of the phenomenon of religion is a question I shall not raise here.)

Our second reaction might be that the religious hypothesis, as James states it, contains expressions of dubious meaning, especially the first affirmation of religion. Why James did not come right out and say that the first affirmation is "A good God exists," or something similar, is not easy to see. Surely this is what must be meant by the "Perfection is eternal" summary. And it is clear from other places in "The Will to Believe" that the right to affirm the existence of God is one of James's concerns, though he always shies away from using the term *God*.[5]

Before considering the question of whether or not the religious hypothesis is a genuine option, I should mention two ways in which the "will to believe" doctrine can be applied to the hypothesis. The first concerns the second affirmation of religion; it might be claimed that this proposition is a W-statement: believing that we are better off believing in the first affirmation might make it come about that we *are* better off believing in the first affirmation. This will obviously depend in part on what is meant by the ambiguous phrase *better off*. But whether or not the second affirmation is a W-statement, the truth of the second affirmation can be seriously questioned, to say the least. It would obviously be very difficult to verify or falsify it unless we made it true by definition, but this would empty it of meaningful content.

On any nontautologous interpretation, there will be a good many nonreligious people who will be prepared to testify against it, for example, by arguing that religious people are not "better off" than they, and so on.

The second point is related to an addition James makes to the religious hypothesis, one that he claims is acceptable to "most of us."[6] It is that the more nearly perfect and eternal aspect of the universe is not an impersonal IT but a personal THOU. (Clearly, James is again talking about God, but the closest he comes to saying so is the term *the gods*.) The point is that if perfection is personal as well as eternal, we must meet the religious hypothesis half-way. Faith can be a way of gaining further evidence that the religious hypothesis is true, for we may be cut off from "making the gods' acquaintance" if we adopt the attitude of the Intellectualist. This, then, is a further example of faith's ability to verify itself.

Whether religious people are "better off" than irreligious people and whether or not religious faith can verify itself are questions we need not try to answer. It *is* important for us, however, to ask whether or not the religious hypothesis constitutes a genuine option. James argues that it does, which does not surprise us, for this is obviously one of the crucial points in his essay. He lets us know early in the essay that his aim is to defend religious faith, and his strategy in doing so should be clear by now. Quite simply, it is that religious faith is epistemologically justified because faith propositions are genuine options.

The religious hypothesis (1) is a live option to most people, James says. That is, most people are willing to admit that it may be true. However, the fact that it is dead to some people will not matter, for James tells us in "The Will to Believe" that he is only speaking to people for whom the hypothesis is live. In addition, the religious hypothesis (2) is momentous in that it obviously involves the possible gain or loss of a great good. James only mentions the "here and now" good involved in religion, but he could also have appealed to the possible good involved in claims of eternal life, rewards in the next life, and so on.

I accept James's argument that religion is momentous and, to most people, live. However, since my view is that the liveness and momentousness criteria can be dispensed with, I will not pause to consider his arguments critically; the remaining two points are the crucial ones. James next argues that the religious hypothesis faces us with (3) a forced option. It is a situation where a decision will be made whether we like it or not: "We cannot escape the issue by remaining sceptical and waiting for more light, because, although we do avoid error in that way *if religion be untrue,* we lose the good *if it be true,* just as surely as if we positively chose to disbelieve."[7] Suspension of judgment is possible here, of course; it is just that the practical consequences of this attitude will be exactly the same as outright rejection, if the religious hypothesis is true.

As we saw in chapter 5, James recognizes only three criteria of genuineness, though he is usually careful to add what I am calling the ambiguity criterion as a separate point. This is what he does here: though he does not explicitly argue for the ambiguity criterion as a fourth criterion, he makes it clear that the evidence for and against the religious hypothesis (4) is "insufficient" to warrant acceptance on evidential grounds alone. The religious hypothesis is not a hypothesis whose truth or falsity is decidable on intellectual grounds.

What are we to make of the case James presents for the genuineness of the religious hypothesis? Let us take the forcedness criterion first. Do the claims of religion face us with a forced option? It seems to me that in certain situations James is correct that they do. Religious issues do sometimes face us with decisions where whatever we do, even if we refuse to decide, we shall in effect make a decision. For perhaps the most basic forced option with which religion faces us is this: either accept the religious hypothesis or do not accept it, that is, either accept what religion will offer you if it is true or go without it. This is not to say, of course, that

since religion faces us with a forced option, we must all commit ourselves wholeheartedly either to religion or to irreligion. This is not the case, for we *can* suspend judgment,
we *can* remain neutral, uncommitted, agnostic. But the point
is, to do so is to choose *not* to accept the religious hypothesis,
and thus run the risk of "losing the truth" if the hypothesis
is true. To decide to suspend judgment on the truth of the
religious hypothesis is in effect to deny it, to refuse to accept
it.

Let us note that there are (at least) three positions we
might take on the issue of the existence of God. We might
affirm God's existence (theism), deny God's existence (atheism), or suspend judgment (agnosticism). James is not
saying that the second position is logically identical to the
third, for this is clearly untrue. What he is saying, however,
it that *practically* speaking, the second and third positions
are identical. For since the religious hypothesis faces us with
a forced option, we must either live our lives as if the claims
of religion were true or live our lives as if they were false.
Both the atheist and the agnostic do the latter, and so the
practical consequences of each position will be the same.
The agnostic is a *practicing* atheist. Religion, then, is a case
where a decision *has* to be made.

But what about the person to whom religion is not a live
option? There seem to be many such people these days, people who just aren't concerned about or interested in religion,
people to whom the question of God's existence is a matter
of indifference. Even they have chosen, James would say.
Their indifference is *in effect* a rejection of the claims of religion. Like the agnostics, they are practical atheists.

But surely there are nonforced options with regard to religion, we want to say here. What about the person who cannot decide whether to become a Christian or a Buddhist?
This is clearly not a forced option, for there are other alternatives with different practical consequences—becoming a
Muslim, for example. It is true that this person faces an avoidable option, and so the "right to believe" doctrine will not
apply to his choice. But surely there is a forced option in back

of his quest: an option all people face, even those indifferent to God. It is this: Either God exists or God does not exist. There are all kinds of definitions of *God* that we could fill in here, and all kinds of religions by which we could express our devotion to such a God as we decided existed. But the option is still forced. And so (if the ambiguity criterion is also satisfied) the "right to believe" doctrine can be used to justify whatever we decide to accept.

Religious faith, James might say, is at its most elemental level an acceptance of God's existence and an attempt to respond to God's existence in some kind of appropriate way. It is this acceptance and this response that the doctrine of the "right to believe" epistemologically justifies.

What, then, about the ambiguity criterion? Can the truth or falsity of the religious hypothesis be decided on evidential grounds? Again we must return to our categorization of evidence situations with regard to the truth or falsity of a proposition p.

(8) No evidence is now available or will ever be available relative to the truth or falsity of p.

(9) No evidence is now available relative to the truth or falsity of p and there will probably never be any.

(10) No evidence is now available relative to the truth or falsity of p but at some time in the future evidence will probably be available.

(11) No sufficient, adequate, coercive evidence is now available relative to the truth or falsity of p. There is only a slight preponderance of evidence for p over not-p (or vice versa).

(12) The evidence for p and against not-p is evenly balanced with the evidence for not-p and against p, i.e., the evidence for p and against not-p is neither stronger nor weaker than the evidence for not-p and against p.

Now the crucial question is, In what category belongs the religious hypothesis? Let us again focus on the proposition "God exists." It is difficult to say where it belongs, and philosophers have differed on the question. (1) Flew and Hare, in their "Theology and Falsification" essays in *New Essays in Philosophical Theology,* seem inclined to place it in category (8), at least as regards *conclusive* evidence. Thus they call the religious hypothesis unfalsifiable. (2) Probably a good many religious agnostics would place the religious hypothesis in category (9). (3) Hick (because of his notion of "eschatological verification") tends to place it in category (10) as concerns *conclusive* evidence, for he argues that while we cannot now know whether or not the religious hypothesis is true, it possibly can (and will, if it is true) be verified in terms of life after death. (James himself seems in places to argue in this manner too.[8]) (4) Several Christian apologists have placed the religious hypothesis in category (11), one of the most notable being Bishop Butler.[9] He argues that there are many cases where adequate evidence is not available and that it is therefore the duty of the mind to commit itself to that view which has the highest degree of probability in its favor, even if the preponderance of evidence over the alternatives is slight. One such case, he claims, is religion: we have no proof that the religious hypothesis is true, but it is more probable than its alternatives. (5) And returning to Hick, it is clear that as regards this life only, Hick would place the religious hypothesis in category (12). For he argues that there is "permissive" evidence for both theism and naturalism, good reasons for and good reasons against each viewpoint. The evidences pro and con are evenly balanced, and thus neither alternative can be verified vis-à-vis the other.

My own view is that the religious hypothesis belongs in either category (11) or category (12). Categories (8), (9), and (10) are excluded because I believe that there does exist a great deal of evidence relative to the truth or falsity of the religious hypothesis. I take it, for example, that the fact that many people have had what they claim to be religious experiences counts in favor of God's existence, and I take it that the presence of natural evil in the world counts against any religious hypothesis that posits a loving and omnipotent God. The only problem is that none of the evidence is definitive or unambiguous: any bit of evidence that might be suggested in favor of or against the religious hypothesis can be (and no doubt has been) challenged. The problem is that the evidence looks like evidence only to those who are already committed to the view that the evidence is said to support. However, evidence does exist, and this rules out (8), (9), and (10). But between (11) and (12) I cannot decide. Perhaps the best thing to say is that the jury is still out. There are some who argue that the balance of evidence, although slight, favors theism, and there are some who make the same claim for atheism. It seems true that there is no *clear* preponderance of evidence in favor of theism over naturalism or vice versa, but whether or not the evidence is exactly balanced is obviously difficult to say.

Based on the conclusions reached in chapter 8, we can say that the ambiguity criterion will be satisfied for the religious hypothesis if the religious hypothesis either belongs in category (12), or belongs in category (11), such that the preponderance of evidence for one alternative over the other is so slight that a rational person basing his decision on the known preponderance of evidence would give him no better chance of making the right decision than basing his decision on his own passions or even on the flip of a coin.

Can the truth of the religious hypothesis be decided on the basis of the present preponderance of evidence (whatever it may be), or can it not? Again, we are going to encounter militant theists and militant atheists who (for once) agree that it can, though for opposite reasons. But it seems to me that the safest conclusion is that it cannot. Witness the fact that there have been truly brilliant minds on both sides of the debate in the history of thought. Witness also the fact (well known to readers of philosophical journals) that seemingly every time somebody comes up with a good argument in support of theism it is soon demolished by nontheists (Malcolm's defense of the ontological argument), and every

time somebody comes up with a good argument against theism it is soon demolished by theists (Findlay's "ontological
disproof"). Perhaps the moral to draw is that if these arguments were demolished, then they were not very good arguments in the first place. Perhaps so. But my point is that none
of the intellectual evidence one way or the other is unambiguous: it is difficult to think of even one theistic or atheistic
argument to which there are not impressive rebuttals. This
is a situation where the truth appears not to be decidable
on intellectual grounds.

It is this kind of situation that the agnostic usually ex-
ploits for his purposes: since the evidence is ambiguous the
best thing to do is suspend judgment. And this is all right
except that the agnostic thinks that the strength of his position is his lofty refusal to decide. But of course he *has*
decided, and if the claims of religion are true, the consequences of his decision will be identical to those of the decision of the atheist.

I conclude that the ambiguity criterion is satisfied in the
case of the religious hypothesis. This means that since both
criteria of the Jamesian case are satisfied, James's "right to
believe" doctrine can be applied to the religious hypothesis.
And this in turn means that the religious hypothesis is a case
where a decision can justifiably be made on some basis other
than evidence.

Let us say that a belief is "epistemologically justified" when
the holding of the belief cannot be criticized on philosophical
grounds, when according to the ethics of belief it is morally
right to hold the belief. As we have seen, James intended
"The Will to Believe" to be a defense of religious faith, and I
have interpreted it as such. But we can see that he was arguing for a general epistemological thesis as well: a thesis
to the effect that our concept of epistemological justification
ought to be broadened. Perhaps I can best point out this thesis by distinguishing among five ways in which it might be

argued that we can be justified in believing a given proposition p.

(1) The Intellectualist, interpreting Russell's Principle as narrowly as possible, declares that we are justified in believing p if, and only if, p is evident. Thus Clifford argues that it is morally wrong to believe any proposition on insufficient evidence. Let us call this "evidential justification." (2) Another philosopher might argue, as James often does in his later works, that we are justified in believing p if believing p is helpful or expedient, if believing p leads to better results than not believing p. I have not stressed this notion in this essay, but it can be called "pragmatic justification." (3) As we have seen, James also often argues that we are justified in believing p if belief in p is self-verifying. We can call this "will to believe justification." (4) A philosopher might also argue that we are justified in believing p if we cannot help but believe in p, if we have no choice in the matter. This might be called "inevitability justification." (As we saw earlier, the "right to believe" doctrine can be interpreted in this way: that in the case of a genuine option we have no choice but to believe as our passional nature directs. I have not stressed this interpretation of the doctrine because I have argued that we *can* suspend judgment in a forced option—though it is true that if the ambiguity criterion is also satisfied, the decision to suspend judgment will itself be a passional decision.) (5) Finally, James argues that we are justified in believing p if p is an alternative of a genuine option. We might call this "right to believe justification."

What James is saying to the Intellectualist is that his notion of epistemological justification is too narrow. In other words, there are other circumstances in which we can legitimately believe p than the circumstance in which p is adequately supported by evidence. Evidential justification must of course remain the foundation of all attempts to gain knowledge; James is not denying this. Nor is he denying that we need to be careful about when and where we allow ourselves to ignore evidential justification in favor of another form of justification. But human experience, life itself, is too broad for us to narrow our epistemological scope as does the Intellectualist. We miss too much this way. Following the Intellectualist leads only to intellectual, moral, religious poverty.

The type of epistemological justification that I have discussed here is "right to believe justification." Whether the other types can be defended by other philosophers in other ways is a question I leave open. But I hope it is clear by now that the "right to believe" doctrine is correct. Whenever a person holds a belief that is an alternative of a genuine option (Jamesian case), whether the belief be a religious belief or not, that belief is legitimate and cannot be criticized on epistemological grounds.

"But surely this is absurd," the critic will want to say here, "surely this gives epistemological license to the holding of all sorts of bizarre and absurd beliefs. Is not James obviously wrong if he deems 'rational' the paranoid's belief that his friends are out to kill him or the religious fanatic's belief that the world will end tomorrow at noon?" The answer to this is that the "right to believe" doctrine does not justify the holding of absurd or superstitious beliefs, for the ambiguity criterion is not satisfied in such cases. James anticipates this objection and emphasizes in reply that the "freedom to believe" he is advocating applies only to options "which the intellect of the individual cannot by itself resolve."[10] The ambiguity criterion is obviously not satisfied in the case of fantastic or superstitious beliefs: the evidence is decisively against these beliefs and so the "right to believe" doctrine has no relevance to them.

I can illustrate James's general thesis in another way, using religion only as the most obvious illustration. It will have been noticed that I have insisted all along that James's "right to believe" doctrine applies to the position of the religious skeptic as well as to the position of the believer. Unlike Pascal's Wager, the force of this doctrine is not that we should adopt religious beliefs, but rather that we have the epistemological right to do so if this is what we want to do. The doctrine also implies that we have an equal epistemological right to refuse to adopt religious beliefs, if that is what we want to do. Thus, as I noted at the end of chapter 7, James's general epistemological thesis can be put in this way: the Intellectualist is wrong when he claims that suspension of judgment is always the only appropriate (epistemologically justified) attitude in cases involving insufficient evidence. In other words, just because a belief is not evidentially justified does not necessarily mean that it is not justified at all.

To return to the application of James's doctrine to religious faith, we can conclude that religious beliefs are legitimate and immune to epistemological criticism (1) if they are alternatives of genuine options (Jamesian cases), and (2) if they are held with an open mind. This means that in such cases the religious skeptic cannot criticize the believer on philosophical (epistemological) grounds. To put it in terms of the ethics of belief, the believer is morally right in believing as he does.

In chapter 6 I noted that the way James develops the liveness criterion seems to imply that only people to whom both the options under consideration are live can use the "right to believe" doctrine to justify their eventual decision. As regards religion, this seemed to rule out both atheists and believers, for to the former religion is surely a dead option while to the latter irreligion is surely equally dead. James's doctrine, then, seems only available to the fence-sitter, the person who has not yet made up his mind.

As we saw in chapter 6, the liveness criterion contains two parts: a hypothesis will be live to a person only if (1) it seems possibly true to him, and (2) it tempts his belief, appeals to him in some way. Now it is true that I did not use this criterion in my amended version of the "right to believe" doctrine, and so I shall ignore condition (2), but there is a sense in which my insistence on "open-mindedness" is close to condition (1). Thus there is a sense in which both the options under consideration must be live to a person before his eventual decision between them can be legitimized by the "right to believe" doctrine. This sense is simply that he must be open to possible evidence on *both* sides. Both alternatives must seem "possibly true" to him, for if one of them does not, he will not be able honestly and fairly to allow his position to be modified should conclusive evidence in its favor become available. I am sure that there are at least some believers who are open-minded in this way, and this would probably be true of some atheists and some fence-sitters as well. So we can conclude that as long as the necessary criteria of the doctrine are satisfied, the "right to believe" doctrine can be used to justify any of these positions on religion. (I will return to this point in chapter 10.)

The criteria must be satisfied, but this does not mean that a person must go through the process of thinking through James's doctrine or even of concluding that his belief counts as an instance of a Jamesian case before his belief is legitimized. As regards the religious believer, it is clear that he will probably not do this. Many believers have never heard of William James, and fewer still understand the "right to believe" doctrine. Furthermore, the believer generally feels no need to question the epistemological standing of his faith; only those believers who feel pressed by the arguments of the skeptic or by their own doubts will have reason to try to justify their faith. The typical believer no more feels a need to justify his faith than he feels a need to justify his love for the members of his family.

But there are believers who are open to their own doubts, and the arguments of the skeptic should be faced squarely. Can religious faith be defended or can it not? It may be that few believers will try to answer this question, but *someone* should. James is one who tries. In "The Will to Believe" he tries to show that the position of religious faith is a philosophically tenable position. And we have seen that James is right: within the narrowly prescribed boundaries he sets, his doctrine can successfully defend religious faith.

NOTES

1. TWTB, p. 11.

2. Miller, "James's Doctrine of 'The Right To Believe,'" pp. 557–58; Hick, *Faith and Knowledge,* p. 42.

3. Robert W. Beard, "'The Will To Believe' Revisited," *Ratio* 8 (December 1966) :178–79.

4. TWTB, pp. 25–26. "The Religious Hypothesis" seems consistent with another hypothesis James discusses in ILWL: that there is "an unseen order of some kind in which the riddles of the natural order may be found explained." ILWL, pp. 51–52.

5. See TWTB, p. 23: "Omniscience only knows . . ."; p. 28: ". . . might cut himself off forever from his only opportunity of making the gods' acquaintance," ". . . obstinately believing that there are gods. . ."; p. 6: ". . . if we were ourselves in the place of the Deity. . . ."

6. TWTB, pp. 27–28.

7. TWTB, p. 26.

8. SR. pp. 95–96, 105–7, 108. Cf. also TWTB, pp. 25, 29–30; ILWL, p. 62.

9. Joseph Butler, *The Analogy of Religion,* ed. W. E. Gladstone, 2 vols. (London: Oxford University Press, 1910) , Introduction, § 4.

10. TWTB, p. 29.

Part III

The Justification
of Religious Belief

Cognitive Meaning

I propose in this chapter to take a new look at an issue in the philosophy of religion that is now some twenty years old, namely, the so-called theology-and-falsification issue.

Religious believers have always assumed that such theological statements as "An omnipotent and loving God exists" were meaningful assertions that describe the world in factual terms. But in 1950[1] Anthony Flew challenged this assumption. In a symposium with R. M. Hare and Basil Mitchell, which was widely read when it was reprinted in *New Essays in Philosophical Theology* (1955),[2] Flew argued that typical theological statements are not assertions at all, that is, they are not the kinds of utterances that can describe the world or that can be either true or false. They assert nothing.

This issue is relevant to the concerns of this study for two reasons. The first is that I have assumed throughout the book what I say that religious believers assume, namely, that theological statements are meaningful assertions about the world. I need, therefore, to show that this assumption is sound. And second, I have made several references to the certainty religious believers typically have that their beliefs are true beliefs. This creates a certain difficulty in showing how James's "right to believe" argument can apply to religious faith (a difficulty I pointed out in chapter 9), and it also raises Flew's problem. We need, then, to answer two questions: (1) Can religious faith be "open-minded" in such a way that the "right to believe" doctrine can be applied to it, and (2) is religious faith, because of its apparent closed-mindedness, open to Flew's charge that faith-statements are cognitively meaningless?

Let us first be clear on the nature of Flew's criticism of theological statements.

We must begin with a definition. Let us say that a statement is an "assertion" and is "cognitively meaningful" if and only if it makes a genuine factual claim about the state of the world, if it is the kind of utterance that can describe how the world is. Thus the statement "The item on the table is a piece of chalk" is a genuine assertion, but "Shut the door!" and "Hurrah for our team!" are not. These utterances describe nothing in the world; the first gives an order and the second vents an emotion. Neither makes a factual claim. They are, then, cognitively meaningless utterances.

Now, the difficulty is that there are some statements that seem to be assertions but that on investigation turn out not to be asssertions. To say that a statement is an assertion only if it makes a factual claim is to say that it is an assertion only if the statement counts for something. And this is a crucial point, for a statement can count *for* something only if it also counts *against* something. That is to say, if an utterance denies nothing, that is, counts against no possible state of affairs, it also asserts nothing. Thus perhaps the simplest way of finding out whether or not a statement is an assertion is to ask whether or not it could be falsified, whether or not any conceivable set of circumstances could show it to be false. We can easily conceive of circumstances that would falsify "The item on the table is a piece of chalk"—for example, looking closer and discovering that it is really a cigarette or section of plastic tubing.

This is where we encounter the difficulty with religious faith, or rather with the statements religious people accept "on faith." For it seems that such statements are typically immune to falsification. Take the statement "An omnipotent and living God exists." Flew claims that this statement denies nothing and thus asserts nothing, because, whatever happens, the believer will not give it up. The typical believer will allow no conceivable event or evidence to falsify his belief in a loving, omnipotent God; for every "evil" event that occurs in the world and is pointed out to him as evidence against his belief, he will suggest a reason why God allowed the event to occur. He will allow nothing to "count against" his belief; his mind is closed; nothing could conceivably make him change his mind. Thus Flew asks the pointed question that has come to be called Flew's challenge: "What would have to occur or to have occurred to constitute for you a disproof of the love of, or of the existence of, God?"[3]

If Flew's question cannot be answered, or if the answer is that nothing could influence the believer to change his mind, then Flew must be correct. Such theological statements as "An omnipotent and loving God exists," which believers had always considered genuine assertions that describe the world in factual terms, are not assertions at all. They are cognitively meaningless utterances, perhaps on the order of swearing or reciting a poem.

This, then, is the falsification challenge. Before launching into the main part of my argument, however, we must note two different claims that are apparently being made here.

The first is that a statement is not an assertion if the person who believes the statement will allow no conceivable contrary evidence to make him reject the statement. Several of Flew's statements read in this way:[4]

... what he would regard as counting against ...

... which would induce the speaker to withdraw it or admit that it had been mistaken.

What would have to occur ... to constitute for you a disproof of. . . ?

What Flew seems to be looking for here might be called a *psychological limit* to belief in a statement. If there is a limit to the contrary evidence that a believer will allow before he modifies his beliefs, the statement he believes is an assertion; if there is no such limit, it is not an assertion. (This has the seemingly odd result that the same statement can be an assertion to one person and a nonassertion to another.)

However, it also appears that Flew is not so much looking for a psychological limit as what might be called an *evidential limit*—a limit of contrary evidence that actually falsifies a statement, a circumstance that, when it obtains, makes it irrational to believe the statement. This notion is not dependent upon the quirks of the individual believer of the statement; when a statement reaches its evidential limit it is presumably falsified for one and all. Thus Flew is saying, on this interpretation of his challenge, that a statement is not an assertion if it has no evidential limit, if no conceivable event or events could disprove it. Assertions, on the other hand, are statements that have evidential limits. Kai Neilsen interprets Flew's challenge in this second way; he says that it amounts to the demand for a "conceivable, empirically determinable state of affairs: which, when attained, falsifies the statement in question."[5]

Flew apparently conflates the two notions of psychological and evidential limit. He asks: "Just what would have to happen not merely (morally and wrongly) to tempt us but also (logically and rightly) to entitle us to say 'God does not love us' or even 'God does not exist?' "[6] The "not merely" clause suggests the notion of a psychological limit, while the "but also" clause suggests the notion of an evidential limit. (I shall return later to the question of the relationship between the two notions in Flew's challenge.)

I intend to make three points in this chapter: (1) that many (if not all) religious believers have a psychological limit to their faith and that the "right to believe" doctrine can therefore apply to their beliefs; (2) that Flew's challenge is unsound and can itself be challenged on all but one interpretation of its meaning; and (3) that if we interpret Flew's challenge in this one sound way, the challenge can be answered in terms of a notion of future verification.

In arguing that religious faith can have a psychological limit, we must first ask what it is about religious faith that tempts people like Flew to consider it immune to falsification. I think that it is clear that this aspect is the *certainty* with which religious faith is typically held. Religious faith usually takes the form of an almost unshakable conviction; it is held with a degree of certainty that seems far to surpass the degree of certainty that the evidence in its favor strictly allows.

No doubt there are several reasons for the degree of certainty displayed by the believer. One reason (which I discussed in chapter 4) would be the fact that religious faith is typically based upon private but very deeply convincing religious experiences that the believer takes to be encounters with God. No one else has experienced my encounters—so the believer might reason—and so it follows that no one else's arguments against my faith can carry any weight. Another would be the fact that the believer in a sense often bases his entire life on his faith; it would be surprising to find a person basing his life on a proposition about which he is uncertain. (Cf. the conviction of a Marxist that Marxism is the best economic system or the conviction of an Irishman that Ireland is a fine country.)

However, I do not see why religious faith cannot be openminded in the way that the "right to believe" doctrine requires, that is, modifiable by possible future evidence. For I think it is entirely possible for a person to base his life on a statement he may later reject. Indeed, this very thing sometimes happens. After all, there are ex-Christians, ex-atheists, ex-Communists in the world who for various reasons of evidence have decided to reject the point of view that once informed their entire existence. It is true that religious faith is normally held firmly, but I do not see why the modifiability requirement must make faith weak or vacillating; I see no reason why a person cannot be firmly convinced of the truth of p and still seek and be open to future evidence on p's truth or falsity as it is discovered in human experience.

Thus James characterizes the faith of the believer in God

and immortality as follows: "He can always doubt his creed. But his intimate persuasion is that the odds in its favor are strong enough to warrant him in acting all along on the assumption of its truth. His corroboration or repudiation by the nature of things may be deferred until the day of judgment."[7] And thus Perry asks: "Who shall say that it is not humanly possible both to believe, and also to harbor saving doubts; both to cast in your lot with one party, and also respect your opponents; both to feel a passionate devotion to your own cause and yet desire to give every cause a hearing; both to believe yourself right and yet acknowledge the possibility that you may be wrong."[8]

Of course we may encounter stubborn religious believers, just as we may encounter stubborn atheists or stubborn Communists, whose beliefs will be without psychological limit. But this does not mean that religious faith is always unmodifiable, that *all* believers have completely closed minds. In fact, it has often been argued on religious grounds that faith is healthier and more authentic if it is open-minded. The point has been made by some theologians that the best kind of religious faith is dynamically involved with doubt; faith needs a kind of healthy skepticism to be genuine. An absolutely certain faith is a dead faith, a static faith, unable to move forward or improve itself. For it is by means of doubt and questions, honestly faced, that the believer moves to a more mature, stronger position of faith.[9]

Thus we can look, for example, at the history of Christianity and see many dogmas that were once accepted as articles of faith but were later rejected because of doubts as to their validity. The medieval doctrine of indulgences was universally accepted in Christendom till Luther raised doubts about it and so triggered the Protestant Reformation. Because of the genealogical calculations of Archbishop Usher, many Christians once believed that the creation occurred in 4004 B.C., but modern science has forced Christians to give up this belief. It could be argued that these and many other examples show a healthy open-mindedness on the part of religious believers, a willingness to abandon or modify statements once accepted on faith when conclusive contrary evidence appears.

However, at this point, a critic would surely raise an obvious objection: "It's all well and good to talk about particular religious beliefs being modified or rejected because of evidence, but what about religious belief itself? This surely is the crucial question. For example, would a religious believer be willing to reject the existence of a good, omnipotent God if contrary evidence became available? Could any conceivable contrary evidence convince the believer that he should modify or give up *this* belief?"

I think the answer to this is yes, at least as regards some religious believers. The faith of some believers may be such that no conceivable contrary evidence would convince them that they should modify their belief (later I shall argue that even this can be questioned) , but we can conceive of contrary evidence that would surely convince many religious believers that they should modify or even reject their belief. For example, it is sometimes said that Christian faith is based upon belief in the doctrine of the bodily Resurrection of Christ. We might wonder, then, how it would affect the faith of Christians if one day an archaeologist were to dig up what overwhelming evidence showed was undoubtedly the body of Jesus, thus disproving the doctrine of the bodily resurrection.

I suspect that if the body of Jesus were to be exhumed, (1) the faith of some Christians might remain unaffected (no matter how strong the evidence, they would reject it) ; (2) some Christians might remain Christians but would retire to an interpretation of Christianity that did not require the doctrine of the bodily resurrection; and (3) some Christians might reject Christianity—and the existence of God—altogether.[10]

In other words, aside from the question whether or not on religious grounds faith ought to have a psychological limit, it seems to me that the faith of at least some believers *does* have a psychological limit. This is not necessarily to say that such believers *will* in the course of their lives change their faith drastically or give it up altogether; for if what they believe is true, that is, if a good, omnipotent God does exist, most probably no evidence will ever count decisively against it. But what I am saying is that there are religious believers for whom we can specify certain conceivable events that would force them to amend or give up their belief. In the case of a Christian, as we have seen, disproof of the doctrine of the Resurrection might do this. For other religious believers, it might force them to do so if human suffering became unmitigated and universal or if someone invented a valid proof of the nonexistence of God based on known premises.

This ought to make us wonder about Flew's phrase "death by 1000 qualifications."[11] He argues that the theist qualifies his religious statements to death, that is, into cognitive meaninglessness, by the fact that he has an answer for any contrary argument the atheist brings up. Thus it soon appears that such religious statements are not genuine assertions, for in his zeal to defend them, the atheist will allow no conceivable evidence to falsify them. But I would deny that what the theist does is come up with "1000 qualifications." So far as I can see he makes only two: (1) he admits that he cannot prove that a good, omnipotent God exists (at least, not to the satisfaction of the atheist), and (2) he admits that he has no answer to the problem of evil (that will satisfy the atheist). So each time the atheist brings up an instance of evil in the world, the believer does not so much add a new qualification as refer back to one he has already made, namely, that for some reason that he admittedly cannot explain, God allows evil to exist.

We can see, then, that there are religious believers whose faith is not without psychological limit.

Let us now take a closer look at the relationship between the notions of psychological and evidential limit in Flew's challenge. As we have seen, some of Flew's statements seem to indicate that he was mainly interested in the second. Perhaps he had both in mind. However, I think we can now see that, whichever he meant, his challenge can itself be challenged. Let us examine the two notions in turn.

(1) Flew's challenge might amount to the claim that theological statements are not assertions because the faith with which they are typically held by believers is without psychological limit. If this is so, my answer is that some believers do have a psychological limit to their faith, and therefore the statements they accept on faith are genuine assertions. (Flew surely cannot be claiming that there are no such believers; the fact that there are ex-believers in the world would refute this claim.)

Flew might then retreat to the weaker position that he was only criticizing those believers whose faith is without limit. This criticism would probably be sound, but surely Flew's language in his "Theology and Falsification" contribution does not support this weaker interpretation of the challenge. Flew seems to be doing much more than just criticizing the stubborn *way* certain believers hold to their faith statements: he seems to be criticizing the faith statements themselves, whoever they are held by and however they are held. This is what makes one think that he is looking for an evidential rather than a psychological limit.

But there is a point that could be raised even against this weaker position. Earlier I tentatively admitted that there may be believers whose faith is without psychological limit and that Flew's criticisms may have some merit as concerns them. But perhaps not even this admission should be made; perhaps the truth is that *every* believer has a psychological limit to his belief. No matter who the believer, no matter what the belief, perhaps there will always be a point of conceivable contrary evidence at which he will be forced to give up his belief. I am not able to argue this point in detail; it would be difficult to know how to establish it. But I mention it because it is perhaps indicative of a confusion that Flew's challenge is based upon. Flew points out, quite rightly, that there are religious believers whose faith has remained steady in the face of all the anti-theistic evidence *that has yet been pointed out to them*. But this does not entail what Flew seems to believe it entails—that the faith of these believers would remain steady in the face of any anti-theistic evidence *that could conceivably be pointed out to them.* Again, I shall not try to argue this point, but simply note that the truth may be that every believer has a psychological limit. It may be just that for the believers Flew had in mind the limit had not been reached.

(2) On the other hand, Flew's challenge might amount to the claim that theological statements are not assertions because they are without evidential limit, because they are such that no amount or quality of contrary evidence could render them false. If this is so, then the question we need to ask of Flew is this: What exactly is an evidential limit? For the notion of evidence disproving or falsifying a given statement is far from clear. It seems to me that there are two possible meanings that might be given to the notion of an evidential limit, but neither will accomplish what Flew intended to accomplish by his challenge.

Perhaps an evidential limit is an amount or quality of contrary evidence so overwhelming in its weight that it would convince anyone beyond a shadow of a doubt that the statement in question is false. In other words, perhaps what Flew is asking for is conceivable evidence against the statement "God exists" that would be clear and distinct and convincing to anybody who noticed it. But of course the problem is that there can be no such evidence for or against any matter of fact. No matter how strong the evidence, the bare possibility of illusion or error can never be ruled out. Furthermore, there are probably going to be people (methodical doubters, perhaps) who will doubt *any* evidence that might come up. So no evidence for or against any matter of fact can be guaranteed to be incorrigible and universally convincing. And if this kind of Cartesian notion was what Flew had in mind, his challenge can surely be dismissed. Religious believers cannot be criticized for failing to specify evidential limits to their faith, for on this definition no statement (outside of logic and mathematics) can have an evidential limit.

But if we reject this definition of an evidential limit, Flew will have to supply us with another, weaker, definition. And it could then be claimed that Flew would be running the risk of collapsing the notion of an evidential limit into that of a psychological limit. Perhaps, after all, an evidential limit is just a psychological limit that has been conventionally accepted as conclusive and final. Perhaps what *proves* (or disproves) a claim about any matter of fact is what *we have simply agreed upon as proving* (or disproving) that matter of fact (where *we* means the community of rational persons). And if this is correct, the obvious difficulty here for Flew is the fact that there are no clear conventions as to what proves or disproves the kinds of theological statements we are considering. In reply, Flew might ask us to attend to the conventionally accepted criteria of proof and disproof for nontheological statements (which ones?) and apply them to theological statements. For instance, he might argue as follows: "An 'evidential limit' is simply the point that is reached when it can legitimately be said that there is adequate evidence that a given proposition is false. Thus someone says, 'The item on the table is a piece of chalk' but, looking closer, we discover that it is really something else. Here we have reached the proposition's evidential limit, for we would have the full epistemological right to say that the proposition 'The item on the table is a piece of chalk' is false."

It seems to me that if any viable sense can be given to the notion of an evidential limit, it will be some such sense as this. However, on this understanding of the notion, theological statements can and do have evidential limits, as I shall argue.

I wish now to raise the so-called notion of *eschatological verification,* a term that has been used by Hick[12] and others to argue that theological statements are cognitively meaningful. In brief, Hick's argument runs something like this: He admits that the statement "God exists" is unfalsifiable (there is no way it could be conclusively disproved), but denies that this means it is not an assertion. For like other statements that cannot be falsified even if they are false ("There are three successive sevens in the decimal determination of pi"), it is a genuine assertion because it can be verified if it is true. Verification and falsification are therefore not symmetrically related. Thus the statement "God exists" may not be falsifiable, but it is an assertion because it can be verified by means of an eschatological experience. (*Verification* for Hick means not "absolute, indubitable proof" but "removal of rational doubt.")

What kind of an eschatological experience? Hick, a Christian, answers that it would be an after-death experience of the reign of Christ in the Kingdom of God. If a person died and then had conscious experiences that included unclouded communion with God as he has revealed himself in Christ and the fulfillment of God's purpose for men's lives, this would effectively exclude all rational doubt about the existence of God and the truth of Jesus' teachings, and so would verify the statements "God exists" and "Jesus' teachings are true." So theological statements can in principle be verified. The issue between the theist and the atheist is a real issue, not a mere verbal or emotional difference, and thus such theological statements as "God exists" are genuine assertions.

Before raising objections to Hick's notion of eschatological verification, we should note that James has in part anticipated some of Hick's arguments. That is, he occasionally writes as if the religious hypothesis could or will be verified. The problem of how it could be verified is a source of perplexity for the reader of James, however. In his discussion of "the religious hypothesis," James says of the first thesis of religion that it "obviously cannot yet be verified scientifically at all." The *yet* seems to imply that it will be verified some day. Beard points out, however, that there is an obvious question that must be asked here: What sort of evidence *could* verify the first thesis? For there are philosophers who would argue that no conceivable evidence could become available that would be relevant to confirming the religious hypothesis. Beard argues that James gives us no answer to this question in "The Will to Believe," that the closest he ever comes to answering it is in the Postscript of the *Varieties of*

Religious Experience, and that the answer James gives there (in terms of the attitude of "prayerful communion") is a weak answer.[13] Similarly, Kaufmann criticizes James as follows: "He writes as if 'the religious hypothesis' were a more or less scientific hypothesis for which no crucial experiment had been devised as yet: one almost gets the feeling that a colleague is working on it even now in the next room, that verification is around the corner, and that we should be stupid if we did not take a chance on it without delay."[14]

These are obviously important criticisms, but it should be pointed out that James has at least a general answer to Beard's question. In his answer James points to the future: he claims that the religious hypothesis will be verified at some time in the future. However, he seems to speak about this future in two ways. Sometimes he gives the impression that at some point in the future the total experience of the human race will have produced enough knowledge to verify the religious hypothesis.[15] It is difficult to understand what James might mean here: What kind of knowledge could be accumulated in later history that (1) is unknown now and (2) would verify the religious hypothesis? (One thinks of knowledge of psychic phenomena—communication with dead spirits, etc. James was interested in this question; could he have meant this?)

However, James also argues in another way, and this is the point I shall emphasize, because it is closer to Hick's approach. He argues that the religious hypothesis will be confirmed at the end of human experience, when all the evidence is in, when the last word will have been spoken. Here are four passages where James speaks in this way:

> When I look at the religious question as it really puts itself to concrete men, . . . this command that we shall put a stopper on our heart, instincts, and courage, and *wait* . . . till doomsday, or till such time as our intellect and senses working together may have raked in evidence enough,—this command, I say, seems to me the queerest idol ever manufactured in the philosophic cave.

The "scientific proof" [that life is worth living] may not be clear before the day of judgment (or some stage of being which that expression may serve to symbolize) is reached.

[The] corroboration or repudiation [of the believer in God and immortality] by the nature of things may be deferred until the day of judgment. The uttermost he now means is something like this: "I *expect* then to triumph with tenfold glory; but if it should turn out, as indeed, it may, that I have spent my days in a fool's paradise, why, better to have been the dupe of *such* a dreamland than the cunning reader of a world like that which then beyond all doubt unmasks itself to view."

For the sake of simplicity I have written as if the verification might occur in the life of a single philosopher,—which is manifestly untrue, since the theories still face each other, and the facts of the world give countenance to both. Rather we should expect, that, in a question of this scope, the experience of the entire human race must make the verification, and that all the evidence will not be "in" till the final integration of things, when the last man has had his say and contributed his share to the still unfinished x. Then the proof will be complete.[16]

James is apparently talking about evidence of human experience in terms of life after death. If so, he has in part anticipated Hick's line of argument, though his point remains undeveloped and vague.

Let us return to Hick's position; it has met with considerable criticism. Some[17] have pointed out that he used theological terms to explicate theological terms. That is, in attempting to show the cognitive meaningfulness of such statements as "God exists," Hick had to resort to such terms as *Christ, God as he has revealed himself in Christ, Kingdom of God,* and *God's purpose for mankind.* But these utterances are themselves open to question. It will first have to be shown that statements in which *they* occur are assertions before they can be used to show that "God exists" is an assertion. So it appears that Hick begs the question: he assumes the assertion status of certain of the very kinds of utterances that he is trying to prove are assertions. Others[18] have argued that the after-life experience Hick postulates is essentially a private experience, and that what is really needed to meet Flew's challenge is public verification. That is, it might have to be admitted that the statement "God exists" would be considered verified by anyone who "experienced the reign of Christ in the Kingdom of God"; but such an experience would not verify the statement for those who have not had the experience.

I note these criticisms of Hick not because I intend to argue about them—I do not know whether or not they refute the notion of eschatological verification—but because they show some of the serious logical difficulties Hick's argument raises. I believe that Hick was on the right track in making his proposal, but I also believe that what he was trying to show can be accomplished in a much simpler way, that is, without appealing to anything so remote as "the eschaton."

Hick was right, I believe, that such theological statements as "God exists" can conceivably be verified, and that they are therefore cognitively meaningful. This is why he focuses on the notion of verification rather than falsification. And I agree with Hick here; he is surely right that verification and falsification are not symmetrically related and that there are statements that are assertions because they can be verified although they cannot be falsified. What, then, does it mean to claim that a statement "can be verified"? Again, I agree with Hick: it means simply that we can imagine logically possible states of affairs that would render the statement immune to rational doubt. Where I disagree with Hick is that I believe it is unnecessary to appeal to the notion of eschatological verification to show that "God exists" can be verified; I intend accordingly to replace Hick's notion with what I shall simply call "future verification." For what is essential to Hick's argument is surely the claim that theological statements *can be verified*: whether this be in the eschaton or simply in the future does not matter. I now intend to argue, therefore, in two different ways, that the statement "God exists" is in principle verifiable in the future experience of mankind.

My first case involves the following bizarre and highly unlikely but logically possible future event: let us suppose that the words *I Exist* (written, say, in Hebrew) one day appeared in the sky in letters of fire in a way that scientists were unable to explain. Would this event verify the statement "God exists"? Well, possibly not; it might still be rationally possible to doubt God's existence; some skeptics would probably claim this, at any rate. But let me point out that since all we need is a logically possible future event—working with the notion of falsification rather than verification, Flew makes it quite clear that the theist can achieve his end by pointing to any *conceivable* event that would falsify his belief[19]—we can make the evidence as strong as we like. We can conceptually combine the astronomical phenomenon described above with all kinds of other evidence for God's existence—evidence a thousand times stronger if we like. Since God is usually claimed to be incorporeal and infinite, the evidence will have to be indirect evidence, but I do not think it difficult to imagine indirect but overwhelming evidence in favor of "God exists." I will let the reader use his own imagination here.

Now the question is, would such events as I have suggested and the reader has imagined verify the statement "God exists"? This of course depends on what is meant by *verify*. If *verify* means something like "prove absolutely" or "prove beyond conceivable doubt," the events would not verify our statement. No doubt there would be skeptically inclined philosophers around who would insist that no matter how strong the evidence, it would fail to amount to verification. For (they might say) the occurrence of the events is logically compatible with God's not existing at all. Again, we immediately think of Descartes here: even if we seem at some future time to experience the imagined events, we could still be "dreaming" them, perhaps because of the machinations of some "Evil Genius."

As a strict logical point this is true. Our events would not verify anything if *verify* means "prove absolutely" or "prove beyond conceivable doubt." But of course outside of logic and mathematics, *verify* means nothing of the sort. As I have noted, no matter of fact can be proved beyond conceivable doubt. The bare logical possibility of error or illusion can never be ruled out. Still, my claim is that the occurrence of the imagined events would constitute such overwhelmingly strong evidence for the truth of "God exists" that it would be irrational any longer to deny the statement. There would no longer be any room for what Hick calls "rational doubt."

This is the only kind of verification that is needed here— and, indeed, the only viable meaning of the word *verify* when we are talking about matters of fact. However, my second case is meant to cover a slightly different and perhaps stronger sense of *verify*. Suppose someone invented a logically valid argument for the existence of God based on known premises. Perhaps the argument could be of some form like

$$1 \qquad \text{I think}$$
$$\cdot$$
$$\cdot$$
$$\cdot$$
$$n$$
$$n+1 \qquad \text{Therefore, God exists}$$

or (cf. the ontological argument)

$$1 \qquad \text{I have an idea of God}$$
$$\cdot$$
$$\cdot$$
$$\cdot$$
$$n$$
$$n+1 \qquad \text{Therefore, God exists}$$

Would such arguments as these verify the statement "God

exists"? It looks as if they obviously would, *ex hypothesi*. And unless there is some reason of logic why such proofs cannot be invented, we must conclude that the inventing of such proofs at some point in the future is a logically possible state of affairs. And if this state of affairs did obtain, it would verify the statement "God exists" in a possibly different and possibly stronger sense of *verify* than we considered above.

Of course if such a proof were invented at some point in the future, we could expect that skeptics would have some objections. Since I am postulating a valid argument based on known premises, neither the argument nor the premises could successfully be challenged. In this case, critics might perhaps appeal to a general argument like Hume's that the existence of no being can be proved: "Nothing is demonstrable unless the contrary implies a contradiction. Whatever we conceive as existent, we can also conceive as non-existent. There is no being, therefore, whose non-existence implies a contradiction. Consequently there is no being whose existence is demonstrable."[20]

If all this did happen—that is, if someone did invent such a theistic proof as I have imagined and if someone else then objected by appealing to Hume's general argument—it would be difficult to know what to say. We would be tempted to say that if the proof is actually logically unimpeachable, the conclusion has to follow and Hume's general argument must be wrong. And, indeed, there are possible difficulties with Hume's argument that could be raised (I will mention one in a moment). Or if we at least agree with the first two sentences of Hume's argument, we might want to say that since the conclusion of our theistic proof ("God exists") *has* to follow, God's nonexistence must be inconceivable, in some sense of the word *inconceivable*. (Supporters of the ontological argument have claimed this very thing.) But on the other hand, a Humean philosopher might want to argue that since Hume's general argument is sound, no such theistic proof as I have imagined is possible, and so we can be sure that no one will ever invent such a proof.

Perhaps the minimum moral to be drawn from this impasse is that we do not now know whether such a theistic proof as we are considering is possible. Of course, it *is* logically possible that someone invent a theistic proof that *seems* to be sound—say, a proof that no logician can at present refute; but on the possibility that Hume's general argument is correct, we would have to allow for the possibility that the argument has some unknown flaw. For if Hume is correct the argument cannot prove what it seems to prove. However, it does seem fair at this point to claim that if such a seemingly sound theistic proof were invented, the burden of the proof would be on the Humean to defend Hume's general argument by showing exactly how the proof is faulty. And if the Humean were unable to do this, then, despite his claim that the proof cannot be sound, I think we should have to consider the proof successful. We might accept the conclusion of the proof, that is, God's existence, with a certain tentativeness because of the bare possibility that the proof will later be shown to be fallacious, but in the absence of this I think that the reasonable conclusion would be to consider that the proposition "God exists" has been verified, that is, made immune to rational doubt.

I mentioned that there are some possible difficulties with Hume's general argument. One difficulty concerns his claim that "Nothing is demonstrable unless the contrary implies a contradiction." Surely Hume is working here with too narrow a notion of what is "demonstrable." His claim requires that only logical truths or tautologies can be demonstrable, for these terms are defined as propositions whose denial is self-contradictory. However, the theistic proofs that I have imagined seem to "demonstrate" God's existence in a different and broader sense than this, and surely it is no violation of ordinary usage to claim that, if these proofs are logically valid and are based on known premises, they do indeed "demonstrate" that God exists. The denial of their conclusion ("God does not exist") will not imply a contradiction, for both my proofs contain major premises that are not tautologies but rather are empirical propositions (that are known to be true) .[21] And since Hume is right that the truth of any empirical proposition can be denied without contradiction, "God exists" can be denied without contradiction. But despite this, I cannot see how it can be denied that such proofs as I have imagined would, if they existed, "demonstrate" God's existence.

Furthermore, even if such proofs did exist, it may still be true, in some psychological sense of the word *conceive*, that I could conceive of God as not existing. In this sense, I can conceive of anything I like, even of the existence of a square circle. But in a more strictly logical sense of the word *conceive*, I can conceive of only what is conceivable, and if square circles are inconceivable because the definition of the term *square circle* is self-contradictory, then I cannot conceive of square circles. Admittedly, even if such proofs as I have imagined did exist, God's nonexistence might still be conceivable (even in the logical sense), for the (empirically true) premises upon which the proofs are based can, like all empirical propositions, be conceived to be false. But again, I cannot see how this has the effect of showing that "God exists" has not really been demonstrated.

I think the proper conclusion is that we can conceive of future states of affairs that would verify the statement "God exists." Thus we can conclude that such theological statements as "God exists" are cognitively meaningful. The statement may not be falsifiable, but this will not turn out to matter. For there are other statements that can be verified if true but that cannot be falsified if false ("There are three successive sevens in the decimal determination of pi") , which I doubt that anyone wants to deny are cognitively meaningful.

So theological statements escape from Flew's challenge on either interpretation of the challenge: first, because some (if not all) religious believers have a psychological limit to their acceptance of theological statements; and second, because the theological statements that were questioned by Flew can conceivably be verified. The first point rules out criticism of theological statements on the "psychological limit" interpretation of Flew's challenge, and the second rules out criticism on the "evidential limit" interpretation. As we have seen, on the only viable understanding of the notion of an evidential limit, the statement "God exists" is an assertion because we can conceive of circumstances[22] in which it would have to be considered verified, in which its negation ("God does not exist") would have to be considered to have reached its evidential limit.

Can the "right to believe" doctrine give an epistemological justification to religious faith? We now have our answer: it justifies those beliefs which (1) are alternatives of genuine options and (2) are held open-mindedly (in the required way). It does not justify beliefs that are not modifiable by possible future evidence (if any are not).

NOTES

1. The "Theology and Falsification" exchange first appeared in the now-defunct journal *University* (1950–51).

2. Anthony Flew and Alasdair McIntyre, *New Essays in Philosophical Theology* (New York: The Macmillan Company, 1964), pp. 96–130.

3. Ibid., p. 99.

4. Ibid., pp. 98, 99.

5. Kai Neilsen, "On Fixing the Reference Range of God," *Religious Studies* 2 (1967):16. Cf. also Flew's statement: "If there is nothing which a putative assertion denies then there is nothing which it asserts either: and so it is not a real assertion." *New Essays,* p. 98.

6. Flew and McIntyre, *New Essays,* p. 99.

7. SR, p. 95.

8. Ralph B. Perry, *In the Spirit of William James* (Bloomington: Indiana University Press, 1958), p. 206.

9. Paul Tillich, *Dynamics of Faith* (New York: Harper and Brothers, 1957), pp. 16–22; Rachel Henderlite, *A Call To Faith* (Richmond, Va.:

John Knox Press, 1961), pp. 19–20. Cf. John Calvin, *The Institutes of the Christian Religion,* ed. John T. McNeill, 2 vols. (Philadelphia: The Westminster Press, 1960), bk. 3, chap. 2, § 4, p. 547: "Unbelief is, in all men, always mixed with faith." Cf. also pp. 654–55.

10. I once attended a theological symposium on the doctrine of the Resurrection, which was addressed by three theologians of widely different persuasions. In answer to the question from the audience, "How would your faith be affected if the body of Jesus were to be exhumed?", each of the above three positions was defended.

11. *New Essays,* pp. 97, 107.

12. Hick, *Faith and Knowledge,* chap. 8; "Theology and Verification," *The Existence of God,* ed. John H. Hick (New York: Macmillan Co., 1964), pp. 253–74.

13. Beard, " 'The Will To Believe' Revisited," p. 173.

14. Kaufmann, *Critique,* p. 118.

15. SR, pp. 105–6, 108. Cf. also TWTB, pp. 27–28.

16. TWTB, pp. 29–30; ILWL, p. 62; SR, pp. 95–96, 107. Cf. also FATRTB, p. 231: "The long run of experience may weed out the more foolish faiths. Those who held them up will have failed: but without the wiser faiths of the others the world could never be perfected."

17. Kai Neilsen, "Eschatological Verification," *Canadian Journal of Theology* 9 (1963) :271–81; D. R. Duff-Forbes, "Theology and Falsification Again," *Australasian Journal of Philosophy* 39 (1961) :152–54; William Blackstone, *The Problem of Religious Knowledge* (Englewood Cliffs, N.J.: Prentice-Hall, Inc., 1963), pp. 114–16.

18. Paul Schmidt, *Religious Knowledge* (Glencoe, Ill.: The Free Press of Glencoe, Inc., 1961), pp. 59–60.

19. *New Essays,* pp. 98, 106.

20. Hume, *Dialogues Concerning Natural Religion* (New York: Hafner Publishing Company, 1948), p. 58.

21. Some would perhaps deny that "I think" is an empirical proposition. I myself do not believe that this statement is true by reasons of logic alone,

but even if it is, the other major premise I mentioned, "I have an idea of God," is surely an empirical proposition and can be taken as the better illustration of my point.

22. It is interesting that Hume himself has Cleanthes conceive of circumstances that might be taken as pointing toward God's existence—circumstances not radically different from my "letters of fire" case. But the use Cleanthes makes of his examples is quite different from the way I have used mine. *Dialogues,* p. 26f.

II

Private Evidence and Skepticism

The concept of private evidence has borne considerable weight in this essay. I have defined faith as "conviction based on private evidence," and I have argued that the evidence a person holds as grounds for his faith-propositions is typically private rather than public. That is, what convinces him that a faith-proposition is true would not necessarily convince anyone else.

But an objection to this analysis of faith is immediately apparent: Does not my use of private evidence simply open the door to the worst kind of arbitrariness in belief? Does it not allow a person whose beliefs are challenged simply to respond, "Well, my (private) evidence convinces me that my beliefs are true, and that's all there is to it, so let's hear no more about it!"?

Thus the aim of this chapter is clear: I will try to discover what (if any) legitimate role private evidence can play in evidence-situations. That is, I will try to answer the question, "Is it ever rational to base conviction on private evidence?" I have already tried to show that in the context of the searching criticisms that philosophical skeptics can raise against some of the most commonly accepted conclusions of general knowledge, private evidence must be used if we are to "know" anything at all. That is, private evidence must be appealed to in general knowledge as well as in religious faith, and so if the "arbitrariness" charge can be made against the conclusions of religious faith, it can also be made against some of the accepted conclusions of general knowledge. My point will be that if it is not dogmatic to use private evidence as the ultimate ground for such a proposition as "The external world exists," then it is not dogmatic to use private evidence as the ultimate ground for such a proposition as "God exists."

Let us return to Russell's Principle. I have argued that there are cases where this criterion of rationality does not apply, and I will continue to argue along these lines in this chapter. Nevertheless, it should be noted that there is a sense in which Russell's Principle is set, established, and agreed upon. I do not believe it would be possible for us to live unless we used the Principle to guide our actions. For anyone who systematically refused to follow Russell's Principle would be very likely to do something foolish, such as leaping in front of a speeding car. For what normally prevents us from leaping in front of speeding cars is our conviction that the proposition "People who leap in front of speeding cars are very likely to be killed" is strongly supported by evidence. And it is Russell's Principle that tells us to believe propositions that are strongly supported by evidence.

But it does seem to me that there are cases where Russell's Principle cannot help us. One such case, as we have seen, is a Jamesian case, that is, a situation where

(1) There is a forced option: I must believe either p or q; there is no third alternative.

(2) The evidence for p and against q is equal to the evidence for q and against p, or no evidence relevant to the truth or falsity of p or q is available.

James's argument in "The Will to Believe," I claimed, amounted to a denial that Russell's Principle always holds. It is precisely in Jamesian cases that James would want to claim that it does not hold, and that therefore we are justified in believing as our passional nature directs.

I believe that a case can be made that, for the religious believer, the proposition "God exists and is at work in the world" constitutes what I called in chapter 3 a "metaphysical belief." His belief in God is constitutive of his entire way of "seeing" the world. For, as Hick says, the person of faith interprets the world in a religious way. He does not differ with the nonbeliever about "the facts": both observe the same events going on in the world. But the believer "sees" the facts in a religious way while the nonbeliever "sees" them in a secular way. In other words, while the believer and the nonbeliever agree on what the facts are (with the exception of purported miracles and other supernatural events, which the believer may accept and the nonbeliever will reject), the believer feels that the facts cannot be adequately explained apart from God, while the nonbeliever feels that they can. So to say that they "see" the world differently is another way of saying that they explain the world (and its significance) differently.

Following James, I will call the believer's "seeing" the world in a religious way "the religious hypothesis" (the hypothesis, we can say, is that God exists and is at work in the world). It was once the case that the religious hypothesis was accepted by most people as a metaphysical belief. But of course this does not show that the religious hypothesis is true, just as the fact that in our era and culture fewer people "see" the world religiously does not show that the religious hypothesis is false. But the question I now wish to ask is: Does the religious believer have the same right to rely on private evidence and "pragmatic considerations" in defending the religious hypothesis as does the ordinary person in defending his knowledge-claims against the philosophical skeptic?

It will be recalled that in chapter 9 I argued that the religious hypothesis can be seen as a genuine option, that is, it is or in certain situations can be an instance of a Jamesian case. I will not argue the point again here. I simply wish to note again that in Jamesian cases it is difficult to see how Russell's Principle is to guide us, or perhaps what should be said is that Russell's Principle does not hold in such cases, and that we can therefore accept propositions on non-evidential bases. Again, it seems to me that this unclarity is in large part responsible for the great disagreement among philosophers whether or not religious faith is ever rationally warranted. As regards the different categories of situations in which it might be claimed that the ambiguity criterion is satisfied (see chap. 9), we can now see that wherever we decide to place the religious hypothesis, we will face extreme difficulty in determining how Russell's Principle is to guide us in deciding whether or not to accept it. (A possible exception is category (11), where Butler is undoubtedly right that we must sometimes decide between two or more options on the basis of only a slight edge in probability, and that in such cases our epistemic duty is to accept that option which is the most probable, even if it is only slightly more probable than the others.) My point then is that with the possible exception of category (11), it is very difficult to say how Russell's Principle is to guide us in deciding what to believe about any hypothesis that is an instance of a Jamesian case. And I have already noted that, while there are grounds for doubting that the religious hypothesis belongs in categories (8), (9), or (10), it would be difficult to say in which of the remaining two categories, (11) or (12), it belongs.

Perhaps this should be a clue to us that much of the long history of the vigorous and often fruitless debate over the extent to which religious faith is or can be "rational" is because religion is one of the areas in which it is difficult to see how Russell's Principle is to guide us, or, if it cannot guide us here, what the relevant criteria of rationality are. This no doubt accounts for the fact that different philosophers have given such widely diverse advice on what to do in such cases. In cases of ambiguous evidence on a proposition p, some (such as James) argue that belief is warranted, some that suspension of judgment is the only rational attitude, and some that actual disbelief is called for.

I have examined James's argument in detail, and need not reopen his case here. He simply argues that in Jamesian cases we can believe either p or not-p and still retain our rationality, that is, acceptance of either disjunct is epistemologically warranted. Anthony Flew is one who argues that the only rational thing to do in such cases is suspend judgment. He denies that, where the truth cannot be known because of balanced evidence,

> the reasonable man must allow the issue to be wide open: six on one side and half a dozen on the other; you cannot prove it and I cannot disprove it. So you can as reasonably choose to believe as I can to disbelieve. Even if there were such a perfect balance of evidence, and that were the whole story, the moral would be: not that belief and disbelief are both reasonable: but that the rational man must suspend judgment.[1]

I have argued against this claim on Jamesian grounds, making use of the notion of a forced option. In a forced option suspension of judgment is pragmatically impossible and so there is no reason to suspend judgment (unless a person fears being in error more than he fears the consequences of losing a possible truth).

Michael Scriven makes the extreme suggestion that in such cases actual disbelief is warranted.[2] Since I have not dealt with this suggestion before in this essay, let us look at his argument. Scriven concludes, after a long and detailed analysis, that none of the traditional theistic proofs is valid and that none of the alleged evidence for God is conclusive. He agrees that there are cases where the lack of adequate evidence for p does not entail not-p, but claims that these cases are restricted to arguments that try to prove p absolutely, without any shadow of doubt. But in cases like the existence of God, where all kinds of evidences and arguments that might produce even a slight probability must be investigated, the situation is different. If a detailed investigation turns up no evidence for God, however slight, then "atheism is obligatory."[3] That is, lacking positive evidence for an entity of which we otherwise know nothing, the only rational conclusion is not agnosticism but atheism.

The absence of such evidence means there is *no* likelihood of the existence of the entity. And this, of course, is a complete justification for the claim that the entity does not exist, provided that the entity is not one which might leave no traces (a God who is impotent or who does not care for us), and provided we have comprehensively examined the area where such evidence would appear if there were any.[4]

Scriven appeals to the analogy of Santa Claus: we have, he says, *no* evidence whatsoever for the existence of Santa Claus, because all the data that once led us as children to believe in Santa Claus (toys appearing under the tree Christmas morning, etc.) can now be explained without any reference to Santa Claus. Thus the proper attitude is not faith that Santa Claus exists, not agnosticism about whether or not he exists, but actual *dis*belief in the existence of Santa Claus. In short, it is foolish to believe a wholly unsupported claim, and the proposition "God exists" is a wholly unsupported claim. Thus the only rational position is atheism.

In response to Scriven, let me first say that it is not quite true that there is *no* evidence for God. It might be argued that there is no *public* evidence for God (I for one would dispute this claim too), but this is quite another thing than to claim that there is no evidence whatsoever for God and that people who believe in God therefore have nothing at all on which to base their belief. Typically, as I have argued constantly in this essay, the believer bases his belief on *private evidence*. So it is false to claim that the typical believer "believes a wholly unsupported claim." Indeed, many believers could produce a great deal of evidence in support of their belief, though the evidence would typically be private in nature—like, say, a religious experience of some kind.

However, the most important point I wish to make against Scriven is still to insist, despite all that he has said, that a lack of evidence for p does not entail not-p. No doubt there are an infinite number of true propositions for which there is not now and probably never will be adequate evidence (or evidence of any kind) available. So not-p simply does not follow from the lack of evidence for p, unless some such proposition as "If p, evidence for p would have turned up by now" can be independently verified.

I take it that Scriven is trying to verify such a proposition in the lines quoted above. This is why he adds the provisos (1) that God must not be a God who has left no traces and (2) that we must comprehensively have examined the entire area where evidences for his existence would have turned up, if in fact he existed. In reply, I must simply point out that there is no guarantee that in his book Scriven has indeed examined all the areas where evidence for God would have turned up if God existed: indeed, since God has typically been described as the transcendent ruler of the entire universe, it is a safe assumption to make that Scriven has *not* examined all the relevant areas. Thus Scriven's provisos are not met, and we can conclude that his defense of atheism fails, that the lack of unambiguous evidence for God does not entail that we must deny God's existence.

The general lines of my strategy for justifying faith-propositions are no doubt already evident. On my view any faith-proposition is justified and I can rationally accept it when:

(3)   It is an instance of a Jamesian case, i.e., I am forced either to accept it or reject it, and its truth cannot be settled on evidential grounds alone.

(4)   It is a belief that for public or private reasons I find more illuminating, i.e., more helpful in explaining my experience than any alternative belief.

I argued in chapter 3 that the major justification for our holding ordinary beliefs that cannot be successfully defended against the philosophical skeptic was our "need" to hold them. We could not live unless we accepted such ordinary beliefs as the belief that jumping in front of speeding cars is dangerous. It might similarly be argued here, then, that the religious believer similarly "needs" to interpret the world religiously—that is, he cannot help himself, he has experiences that he cannot interpret in any other way than in terms of God, and he simply "finds himself" interpreting the world religiously. Now this may or may not be an accurate description of the experience of the typical religious believer (I think it is), but the believer's "need" to interpret his experience religiously is surely not exactly like the ordinary person's "need" to hold his ordinary beliefs. For while it is not possible to live apart from such ordinary beliefs as we all accept, it certainly is possible to live without interpreting the world religiously. Atheists and agnostics are not forced to "lie down and die."

But I still claim that the religious believer is justified in accepting such faith-propositions as "God exists and is at work in the world," for such a proposition constitutes for him a metaphysical belief held in the context of a Jamesian case for which he has convincing private evidence. He can rightly claim, "My world would be a significantly different world without God," just as the ordinary person can claim, "My world would be a significantly different world apart from my belief that things retain their continuity in time."

So what I am saying is that, where we cannot settle the question of the truth of a belief on public evidential grounds, and where the exigencies of life are such that we must choose either to accept or reject it, then the only criterion left to which to appeal is private evidence. One such way to decide, for example, is to ask: Which alternative is ultimately more illuminating to me? This appeal to "illumination" is, I take it, usually private (although doubtless in some cases there are public criteria that one thesis or theory is more illuminating than another); normally, what is illuminating to me need not be illuminating to you. I suspect that this is the only sort of justification (other than "need") that can ever be given for *any* metaphysical belief, whether it be religious or secular. That is, the only argument left when the public evidence is seen to be ambiguous is to claim: "I am simply better able to explain my life, my experience, my world on the basis of this assumption than on the basis of any other." And as we saw earlier, this is the kind of move we all make in questions of general knowledge when we are confronted with skeptical challenges that we cannot answer. What I am claiming is that we are justified in behaving similarly in relation to religious beliefs. If this is arbitrariness in belief, then it follows that we are all of us arbitrary.

Now, I do not want to imply that the situation is exactly analogous between the use of private evidence to justify ordinary and metaphysical beliefs in the context of general knowledge and the use of private evidence to justify religious propositions. I am not claiming that all the ordinary and metaphysical beliefs that I listed in chapter 3 count as Jamesian cases. For despite the fact that there are skeptical questions about each belief that we cannot answer apart from pragmatic considerations, I (a nonskeptic) would want to maintain that the available evidence in most cases clearly supports them. But this is not the case with such a religious belief as "God exists and is at work in the world," for here the evidence is ambiguous, and we are therefore involved in a Jamesian case. Nevertheless, I do not think that this disanalogy refutes my argument, for the crucial part of the analogy still remains: the fact that, in either case, any purported bit of evidence can be challenged by the philosophical skeptic in such a way as to force an appeal to private evidence in order to stop debate. For example, let us take the metaphysical belief "Things retain their continuity in time." There is evidence for this belief, but not the kind of evidence that adequately answers the skeptic's questions. For as I suppose, the major evidence in support of this belief is the fact that things appear to us to retain their qualities over periods of time: when I perceive a pencil, momentarily look away, and then perceive the pencil again, the pencil appears not to have changed, it appears to be the same pencil. Thus "Things retain their continuity in time." But of course this kind of evidence can easily be challenged by the skeptic: he can simply ask, How do you know it is "the same" pencil?

Now it is possible for the religious believer to doubt that his experience is experience of God, just as it is possible for the philosophical skeptic to challenge any ordinary knowledge-claim by asking, "How do you know. . . ?" But as we learned from Peirce, the mere ability to replace the period at the end of a sentence with a question mark does not give us ground for doubt. In reply to the nonbeliever's challenge that his faith may be ill-founded, the believer can simply say what the ordinary person can say to the philosophical skeptic: I am convinced of what I believe, and *I shall continue to believe till you give me good reason not to believe.*

How do the pragmatic considerations I spoke of in chapter 3 enter in here? They are relevant to decisions to be made in Jamesian cases in two ways: (1) Where an option I face is forced, I admittedly have the logical freedom to decide not to decide, but for pragmatic reasons I see that not deciding is equal to deciding for one of the alternatives. That is, the results will be the same, and so (for pragmatic reasons) I see that I *must* decide; whatever I do, it will *in effect* constitute a choice of one of the alternatives. (2) Where, in addition to this, the evidence is ambiguous, I have the epistemological right to choose the option I will choose on the basis of pragmatic reasons. That is, I can decide on the basis of my hopes and desires if I decide to choose on that basis. Or (if this is different from the first) I can choose to accept a hypothesis just because for private reasons I find it more compelling or more able to explain and illuminate my experience than any alternative hypothesis.

In this penultimate section I will attempt to draw some thoughts together that run across the various topics with which I have dealt in this essay. Let me first borrow the term *intellectualism* from James and define it much more briefly than he did. Let us simply say that *intellectualism* is the view that Russell's Principle holds in all evidence-situations. Thus, on intellectualism, believing a proposition for which there is inadequate evidence is always forbidden (as W. K. Clifford, in his dictum, explicitly says). How is intellectualism related to skepticism? I do not claim that intellectualism is the same position as philosophical skepticism, either Sextus's form of skepticism or what I called adequate skepticism. But it does seem clear that intellectualism reduces to skepticism if it is true, as I concluded, that all knowledge is based on faith. If knowledge cannot be had without believing nonevident propositions (i.e., without having faith), and if faith is forbidden (intellectualism), then no knowledge-claim can be substantiated (skepticism).

But if skepticism seems an unacceptable position, as it does to me, then intellectualism must be rejected. Intellectualism can rationally be rejected if it can be shown that faith (belief based on private reasons) can legitimately be used in evidence-situations. I believe that reasons can be given for the claim that faith is sometimes rationally warranted and can be so used. These reasons are pragmatic reasons: we need to know or at least to have rational beliefs in order to live, and if faith is necessary to knowledge or to rational belief, then faith is warranted. Of course "believing p for pragmatic reasons" is not exactly the same thing as "believing p on faith." I do not claim that the two always are or need be the same, but the obvious connection is that both are instances of "believing p without adequate public evidence that p."

An objection to this might be raised as follows: "If what constitutes adequate evidence is ultimately determined by the consensus of rational persons, then what if the consensus of rational persons says that skepticism is wrong because we do indeed know p, where p is, say, 'Davis is now holding a pencil in his hand' "? But the answer to this is that while consensus is the ultimate determiner of whether or not evidence is adequate, consensus cannot determine whether or not someone is in a state of knowledge. Gettier's counter-examples show that I may have adequate evidence for p and yet not know p. Simply because I have adequate evidence for p does not mean that I know p—unless it can also be shown (1) that I believe p and that p is true, and, more important, (2) that the traditional analysis of knowledge (in some form) is sound. And we saw that grave doubts can be raised about this analysis even apart from Gettier.

What I have argued in this essay is that philosophical skepticism cannot be refuted, but cannot be lived, either. Thus nonphilosophical reasons must be found for rejecting it, that is, for believing propositions that we cannot show that we know. What I have claimed is that we can believe p without adequate evidence for p (i.e., we can have faith that p or believe p on private evidence) when there is a compelling pragmatic need to believe p or when the situation is a Jamesian case. This, I claim, shows the falsity of intellectualism. And this result applies not only in general knowledge but in religion as well: I can believe on faith a given theological proposition q if the situation is a Jamesian case and if I have convincing private evidence for q—like, say, a mystical experience of some sort or a realization that q illumines my experience in a compelling way.

To repeat, where the truth of a belief cannot be settled on evidential grounds and where a person must choose either to accept or reject it, a rational person is justified in accepting for public or private reasons that belief which he finds most illuminating, which he is able to use to make the most positive significance for his life. This does not show that the belief is true—only that it is rational to accept it. If public evidence later becomes available that refutes the belief, then obviously the rational thing to do will be to reject it. But it is not rational to reject it just because there are questions about it that we cannot answer; otherwise it would be rational to reject all our ordinary beliefs. We have all learned to live with unmet challenges in questions of knowledge, and I see no reason to rule that we cannot behave similarly in questions of religion.

This, then, answers the question with which I began this chapter: It is sometimes rational, it is sometimes justified, to base conviction on private evidence. That is to say, a rational person can also be a person of faith, a person who interprets his life, his experience, and his world in terms of God.

To conclude this study, let me make some general comments on what I perceive to be the value of this theory of faith and its epistemological justification, why I find it a helpful and illuminating way of looking at religious faith.

First and most important, I think that my view correctly describes the phenomenon of religious faith as it can be seen in the lives of religious people. For I think such people do believe for reasons that are subjectively convincing but objectively inadequate. There are reasons why they believe: believers can produce evidence; but this evidence is private in that it would not typically persuade other people to believe. Second, I believe that my view is not overly fideistic: I have insisted that faith is based on evidence and my theory does not allow the holding of irrational or superstitious beliefs. Belief beyond evidence is justified by my theory only in cases of genuine options, and the ambiguity criterion rules out absurd or ridiculous beliefs. But third, I do not think that my view is overly rationalistic, either. Within the carefully prescribed limits I set, it is safe to say that my theory allows for what might be called a sort of subjectivism. And there is no reason why the kind of faith I have mainly described in dry epistemological terms cannot also be a faith toward God of full religious commitment, trust, and obedience.

I hope that my theory of religious faith is illuminating to at least three sorts of people. (1) I hope that it speaks to those religious skeptics who cannot understand how anyone could be foolish enough to believe in things that cannot be seen or touched or proved; to such people as W. K. Clifford, who regard faith as somehow immoral, I hope that they can now see why religious believers feel free to believe as they do. (2) I hope that it also speaks to religious believers of uneasy conscience who dishonestly keep their doubts repressed, who fear that any truly rational person ought to give up religious faith. I hope that they can now see that their doubts ought to be faced squarely and that religious faith can endure even in the teeth of the most rigorous questions of the religious skeptic. (3) Finally, I hope that it speaks to those nonbelievers who long for religious faith and the hope and peace it can bring but whose intellectual scruples prevent them from making any sort of faith commitment. I hope that they can now see that, at least as regards the sort of religious faith I have been describing, philosophy need not prevent faith.

At any rate, for the Christian, the ultimate verification of his faith is that it dovetails with his ordinary beliefs about the world and it illuminates his entire experience in a new and compelling way. With one exception, I believe Hick is correct when he says that the believer and the nonbeliever do not differ in the facts that they see and affirm in the world; their disagreement is limited to the proper interpretation to place on these facts. The exception is in the realm of the miraculous: The Christian believer will hold that certain miraculous events have occurred in history, for example, the Resurrection of Jesus Christ from the dead, while the nonbeliever will not allow that any such events have occurred. But beyond the few instances of miracles or purported miracles, the believer and the nonbeliever see the same events unfolding in human experience but interpret them differently. For example, if they successfully pass through a difficult period of trouble, one may well attribute it to God's grace while the other will view it as a natural event. If a piece of good fortune strikes, one may attribute it to answered prayer and the other to sheer coincidence. For the Christian, then, what ultimately convinces him of the soundness of his faith is that it creates for him a world view, a perspective from which to interpret all of his experience, a perspective that explains and illuminates the events of his life in a way that he finds compelling.

NOTES

1. Anthony Flew, *God and Philosophy* (London: Hutchison and Company, 1966), pp. 193–94.

2. Michael Scriven, *Primary Philosophy* (New York: McGraw-Hill Book Company, 1966), pp. 102–7, 156–67.

3. Ibid., p. 103.

4. Ibid., pp. 102–3.

Bibliography

Aquinas, Thomas. *On the Truth of the Catholic Faith (Summa Contra Gentiles)*. Garden City, N.Y.: Hanover House, 1955–1957.

Beard, Robert W. " 'The Will To Believe' Revisited." *Ratio* 7 (December 1966).

Bendall, K., and Ferre, F. *Exploring the Logic of Faith*. New York: Association Press, 1962.

Blackstone, William. *The Problem of Religious Knowledge*. Englewood Cliffs, N.J.: Prentice-Hall, 1963.

Clifford, W. K. *Lectures and Essays*. Vol. 2, edited by Leslie Stephens and Frederick Pollack. New York: Macmillan and Company, 1901.

Craig, Charles H. "A Layman's Definition of Faith." *The Review and Expositor* 49 (April 1952).

Ducasse, C. J. *A Philosophical Scrutiny of Religion*. New York: The Ronald Press, 1953.

Duff-Forbes, D. R. "Theology and Falsification Again." *Australasian Journal of Philosophy* 39 (1961).

Flew, Anthony. *God and Philosophy*. London: Hutchison and Company, 1966.

———, and MacIntyre, Alasdair. *New Essays in Philosophical Theology*. New York: The Macmillan Company, 1964.

Fogelin, Robert J. *Evidence and Meaning*. London: Routledge & Kegan Paul, 1967.

Gettier, Edmund L. "Is Justified True Belief Knowledge?" *Analysis* 23 (1963).

Hallie, Philip P. *Scepticism, Man, and God: Selections from the*

Major Writings of Sextus Empiricus. Middletown, Conn.: Wesleyan University Press, 1964.

Hare, Peter H., and Madden, Edward H. "William James, Dickinson Miller, and C. J. Ducasse on the Ethics of Belief." *Transactions of the Charles Peirce Society* 4 (Fall 1968).

Hick, John. *Faith and Knowledge.* 2d ed. Ithaca, N. Y.: Cornell University Press, 1966.

———. *Philosophy of Religion.* Englewood Cliffs, N.J.: Prentice-Hall, 1963.

———, ed. *The Existence of God.* New York: The Macmillan Company, 1964.

Hume, David. *Dialogues Concerning Natural Religion.* New York: Hafner Publishing Company, 1948.

———. *An Enquiry Concerning Human Understanding.* LaSalle, Ill.: The Open Court Publishing Company, 1946.

———. *A Treatise of Human Nature.* Oxford: The Clarendon Press, 1965.

James, William. *Collected Essays and Reviews.* New York: Russell and Russell, 1920.

———. *Some Problems of Philosophy: A Beginning of an Introduction to Philosophy.* New York: Longmans, Green, and Company, 1911.

———. *The Will To Believe and Other Essays in Popular Philosophy.* New York: Dover Publications, 1956.

Kant, Immanuel. *Critique of Pure Reason.* Translated by Norman K. Smith. New York: St. Martin's Press, 1965.

Kaufmann, Walter. *Critique of Religion and Philosophy.* Garden City, N.Y.: Doubleday and Company, 1961.

Kennedy, Gail. "Pragmatism, Pragmaticism, and the Will To Believe—A Reconsideration." *The Journal of Philosophy* 55 (1958).

Kierkegaard, Søren. *Concluding Unscientific Postscript.* Translated by David F. Swenson. Princeton, N.J.: Princeton University Press, 1941.

Locke, John. *An Essay Concerning Human Understanding.* Edited by Alexander Fraser. 2 vols. Oxford: The Clarendon Press, 1894.

Macleod, William. "James's 'Will To Believe': Revisited." *The Personalist* 47 (1967).

Matson, Wallace I. *The Existence of God*. Ithaca, N.Y.: Cornell University Press, 1965.

Mavrodes, George. "James and Clifford on 'The Will to Believe.'" *The Personalist* 44 (1963).

Miller, Dickenson. "James's Doctrine of 'The Right to Believe.'" *The Philosophical Review* 51 (1942).

———. "'The Will To Believe' and the Duty to Doubt." *International Journal of Ethics* 9 (1898–1899).

Neilsen, Kai. "Eschatological Verification." *Canadian Journal of Philosophy* 9 (1963).

———. "On Fixing the Reference Range of God." *Religious Studies* 2 (1967).

Newman, John Henry Cardinal. *An Essay in Aid of a Grammar of Assent*. Garden City, N.Y.: Image Books, 1955.

Pascal, Blaise. *Pascal's Pensées*. New York: E. P. Dutton and Company, 1958.

Peirce, Charles S. *Charles S. Peirce: Selected Writings*. Edited by Philip P. Wiener. New York: Dover Publications, 1958.

Perry, Ralph B. *In the Spirit of William James*. Bloomington: Indiana University Press, 1958.

———. *The Thought and Character of William James*. Vol. 2. Boston: Little, Brown and Company, 1935.

———. *The Thought and Character of William James: Briefer Version*. New York: Harper and Row, 1948.

Popkin, Richard. "David Hume: His Pyrrhonism and His Critique of Pyrrhonism." In *Hume,* edited by V. C. Chappell. Garden City, N.Y.: Anchor Books, 1966.

Russell, Bertrand. *A History of Western Philosophy*. New York: Simon and Schuster, 1945.

Santayana, George. *Character and Opinion in the United States*. New York: Anchor Books, 1956.

Schmidt, Paul. *Religious Knowledge*. Glencoe, Ill.: The Free Press of Glencoe, 1961.

Scriven, Michael. *Primary Philosophy*. New York: McGraw-Hill Book Company, 1966.

Sextus Empiricus. *Against the Logicians*. Translated by R. G. Bury. Cambridge, Mass.: Harvard University Press, 1935.

———. *Outlines of Pyrrhonism*. Translated by R. G. Bury. Cambridge, Mass.: Harvard University Press, 1933.

Index